SELECTED ISSUES
— *in* —
RELIGIOUS LAW

Patrick J. Cogan, S.A., Editor

Bulletin on Issues of Religious Law
1985-1995

© 1997 by Canon Law Society of America

ISBN 0-943616-74-3

SAN 237-6296

All rights reserved. No part of this book may be reproduced in any manner without the permission of the copyright holder, except for brief quotations in critical reviews and articles.

Canon Law Society of America
The Catholic University of America
Washington, DC 20064

TABLE *of* CONTENTS

FOREWORD 1

I. GOVERNANCE
   1. Questions Asked by the Congregation for Institutes
      Of Consecrated Life and Societies of Apostolic Life 4
      Margaret Mary Modde, O.S.F.
   2. What is Meant by the "Personal Authority"
      of Religious Superiors? 10
      Sharon Holland, I.H.M.
   3. Can a Religious Institute Adopt a Collegial Form
      Of Government? 12
      Ellen O'Hara, C.S.J.
   4. Is it Permissible to Have Direct Election (Non-chapter)
      Of Supreme Moderators and Major Superiors? 15
      Ellen O'Hara, C.S.J.
   5. Election of Major Superiors 17
      Rosemary Smith, S.C.
   6. Laity and the Power of Governance:
      A Statement of the Question 26
      Sharon Holland, I.H.M.

II. ADMINISTRATIVE ISSUES
   7. Vocational Crisis 34
      Fred Sackett, O.M.I.
   8. Indefinite Leave of Absence 36
      Fred Sackett, O.M.I.
   9. Complementary Competencies: Bishops, Superiors,
      And Apostolates 38
      Richard A. Hill, S.J.
   10. Dispensation and Dismissal 42
       Elizabeth McDonough, O.P.
   11. Selecting a Canonical Advisor 48
       James H. Provost
   12. The Merger and Union of Religious Institutes 50
       Melanie Bair, O.S.F.
       Jordan Hite, T.O.R.

13. Dealing with the Difficult Religious 57
    Rose McDermott, S.S.J.
14. Transfer to Another Institute — Canons 684-685 66
    Rose McDermott, S.S.J.
15. Relationship Between Bishops and Religious:
    Mutual Rights and Duties 69
    Elizabeth McDonough, O.P.
16. Associate Membership in Religious Institutes 77
    David M. Hynous, O.P.
17. Canon 702, §2 — Equity and Charity to Separated Members ... 85
    Rose McDermott, S.S.J.
18. Recent Developments in Consecrated Life 92
    Rose McDermott, S.S.J.
19. Sponsorship 101
    Madeline Welch, O.S.U.
20. Clerics and Religious in Public Office:
    Prohibitions in Canon Law 113
    Claudia Barbre, R.S.M.

III. CONFIDENTIALITY

21. The Issue of Confidentiality in Religious Life 124
    Francis G. Morrisey, O.M.I.
22. Confidentiality Issues Regarding a Religious Institute
    and its Relationships with a Diocese 135
    Francis G. Morrisey, O.M.I.
23. The Individual's Right to Confidentiality 142
    Elissa Rinere, C.P.

IV. NOVITIATE

24. Purpose and Place of the Novitiate: Canons 646 – 647 150
    Rose McDermott, S.S.J.
25. The Inter-Community Novitiate 154
    Jordan Hite, T.O.R.
26. Admission to the Novitiate: Canon 643, §1, 2° —
    Impediment of Existing Marriage Bond 160
    Rose McDermott, S.S.J.

AUTHORS 163

INDEX 164

Foreword

The *Bulletin on Issues of Religious Law* is a collaborative project of the Canon Law Society of America, Conference of Major Superiors of Men, Leadership Conference of Women Religious, and the National Conference of Vicars of Religious. Published bi-annually, the *Bulletin* is a resource for issues in canon law which have direct relevance for or impact upon religious institutes. This volume is a compilation of the entries of the *Bulletin* for the period of 1985-1995 in order to facilitate their location and retrieval. The contributors have revised and updated their entries since original publication.

Patrick J. Cogan, S.A.
Editor

I.
Governance

1.
QUESTIONS ASKED BY THE CONGREGATION FOR INSTITUTES OF CONSECRATED LIFE AND SOCIETIES OF APOSTOLIC LIFE

Since 1977 I have facilitated religious here and abroad in the writing of their proper law. Through the use of a process which involved the total community in writing its law, most of the communities completed — within two to three years — final drafts of their constitutions and the directives for their practical implementation. Some of the communities also completed a set of administrative policies in the areas of elections, formation, ministry, governance, and finance.

Of the seventy-some communities I worked with, most have received at least a first critique of their constitutions from the Congregation for Institutes of Consecrated Life and Societies of Apostolic Life (CICLSAL). These reviews have presented observations ranging in number from four to over 150 items: suggestions to bring the community's law into closer conformity with the law for the whole church. Through response to these observations, either by way of acceptance of changes recommended by CICLSAL, or by way of explanation of certain points, over one-third of the communities now have church approval.

Communities who are still in the process of writing their proper law, and communities who have not yet received approval of their constitutions and directives, are curious about the observations CICLSAL makes. Some have heard from various sources that these observations are, at least in part, restrictive for the life of a community, or narrow in their integration of the changes initiated by Vatican II, or inconsistent in their interpretation of the code and its requirements for consecrated life. Some respond negatively to what they have heard and lose hope for the value of proper law, or for the possibility of recouping group energies for what they see as weightier and more worthwhile tasks of church ministry. Some institutes, which held pre-code church approval and which were required to update items not in conformity with the code, feared revival of conflicts within their communities on meanings and preferences concerning certain behaviors which their experience suggests are inconsequential for a healthy community life and ministry.

An analysis of the observations made by CICLSAL may be useful to such communities. For some it may dispel fears of revived conflicts. For others it may recall broad directives initiated by Vatican II to support the hopes of the Christian faithful. For still others it may provide a concise description of the Church's current view of consecrated life and a brief indication of possibilities for further affirmation, renewal, or change in religious life. For those who find the law unnecessary, unmanageable, inconsistent, or restrictive, an analysis can be helpful to sustain the dialogue initiated by Vatican II in the Constitution on the Church. Especially these latter should view professionally the observations of CICLSAL, and their various analyses, regarding them not as legal imperatives but as questions CICLSAL asks.

Keeping in mind the overall purpose of my analysis, I will divide the questions CICLSAL asks into two areas: the first on overall composition, the second on necessary norms. In both areas I will present a general summary of the observations CICLSAL makes before suggesting the underlying questions. I will conclude with an analysis of the broader framework of church law within which CICLSAL seems to operate.

I. Questions of Overall Composition

In general, it should be noted that CICLSAL examines the constitutions of a community in conjunction with the community's directives for their implementation. Each article in both documents is to be numbered, those of the first document consecutively throughout, those of the second, preferably, with numbers corresponding to the companion article in the constitutions. Each document as a whole and each article in particular is examined, as any writing, for its brevity, clarity, inherence, and completeness.

To assure the brevity of the documents, CICLSAL discourages prefaces, appendices, quotations, citations, and unnecessary topics. Brevity is achieved through elimination of repetitions, floridities, lengthy explanations, and unnecessary details. On the whole CICLSAL accepts any orderly format for the documents. Whether or not there are divisions or chapter titles or sub-titles depends entirely on the community. Full-page, half-page, or broken lines to present statements, and the comparative length of chapters, sections, articles, or items, or their parts, again is the choice of the community. On occasion CICLSAL has observed that a community's explanation of its basic beliefs is too sketchy and should be further developed. On other occasions, CICLSAL has discouraged the division of constitutions and directives into books or further parts, or has noted a general tendency to be profuse.

Clarity of a statement, concept or term frequently elicits comment by CICLSAL. Often a re-phrasing is suggested, or a precise term or word supplied. If the presentation of a certain concept is unclear, a general question on its meaning is raised. On the whole CICLSAL suggests simple words, classical terms for religious life, and concepts of religious life which have their origin in *Perfectae caritatis*. In particular, CICLSAL specifies perpetual profession for perpetual vows; the renewal of baptismal commitment rather than covenant with God as the basis for vows; the designation novice, sister, brother, or cleric rather than member; the designation superior rather than coordinator, moderator, or similar referents; and the designations council, chapter, province, and region rather than more recent modifications or changes in these referents naming traditional groups or parts of a community.

Inherence in the documents concerns their inner logic of parts, sequences, and ideas. CICLSAL looks for the name, or title, of a community in the first item of the constitutions, and an exact indication of whether the community is pontifical or diocesan; contemplative or apostolic; religious, secular, or societal; indigenous or international; of sisters, brothers, clerics, laity, or a mix of these; and endowed with a specific charism and ministry. Against this basic identity of the community the norms of belief and behavior which follow in a community's law can be tested for their propriety. In particular, CICLSAL carefully examines the wording of a community's formula for vows, or, if these do not exist in the tradition of the community, the wording for other specific bonds with the Church. No matter the fact of vows or other sacred bonds, each community is carefully checked for its understanding that everyone who chooses close ties with the Church through a community is obligated to participate as fully as possible in the chastity, poverty, and obedience of Christ as articulated in the constitutions of the particular community chosen.

Completeness of the documents revolves on the community's inclusion of its beliefs and behaviors in areas integrally related to their fuller participation in the chastity, poverty, and obedience of Christ. To support this choice certain structures are necessary for prayer, for ministry, and for the exercise of authority by the community in the Church and by certain individuals in the community. Representatives of CICLSAL, and canonists in general, consequently suggest treatment of a community's beliefs and behaviors in the following inter related topical areas: consecrated life, chastity, poverty, obedience, prayer, community, ministry, formation, and governance. Governance ordinarily treats smaller communities, major parts, superiors, councils, chapters, assemblies, secretaries, and treasurers of a community. Often included in the section, but occasionally in separate sections, are the community's requirements for beliefs and behaviors on the administration of temporal goods, separation from the community, and obligations to the constitutions.

Underlying CICLSAL's observations on the overall composition of constitutions for a community is the basic question of a community's sure grasp of its identity: Who am I? Whether the question is answered by an individual or by a community, the pith of the answer is determined by an interplay of the realities of individual, communal, and ecclesial awakenings, visions, experiences, dreams, perceptions, hopes, histories, and determinations. Of all these elements, law especially unites the latter four.

II. Questions on Necessary Norms

Topical inclusions in constitutions are further complemented by the code's requirements for inclusion of certain norms. Of the 174 norms on consecrated life, over one hundred of them direct communities to include certain details in their proper law. In addition, other sections of the code are important for determining exact details a community needs in writing its law on elections, initiating new forms of ministry, administering property, and seeking indults and dispensations.

To draw up a complete list of necessary norms challenges individual and communal expertise, sharpness, patience, and ego-strength! CICLSAL has an unofficial list for private use which helpfully and succinctly notes nine topics and some 160 details, together with the relevant canons. From critiques various communities have received, another hundred or so subtle details could be added. Such details may not be literally stated in the code. They proceed from studied perspectives on the Church, its law, its guidance of the choice for consecrated life, its overall mission, and the established identity of the community seeking approval.

To summarize briefly the norms CICLSAL requires of communities, it seems best to group the basic topics. From these topical groups a brief analysis can then be suggested. A first grouping would include the topics of consecrated life and its core of chastity, poverty, and obedience. The second grouping would gather prayer, community, ministry, and formation as the integral supports for consecrated life. The third grouping would treat governance, administration of goods, separations, and obligations to constitutions as general supports for consecrated life.

In accord with the norms of the code and the questions CICLSAL asks, consecrated life is a choice freely made. It is a response to God's invitation to live in community with others who seek the fullness of charity through a specific way of gospel life. For those who choose this way of life, chastity consists of celibacy and continence for the sake of the kingdom announced by Christ.

Poverty consists of foregoing the independent administration, use, and benefits of the goods one owns—namely one's patrimony—specifying in a will who receives ownership when one dies, and, in addition, giving over to the community the goods one subsequently earns or receives, then living simply as determined by the norms the community sets down for itself.

Obedience consists of learning God's will in one's own regard specifically through obedience to those in the community elected or appointed for the exercise of authority, and through personal obedience to the pope. CICLSAL places practical emphasis on the baptismal foundation of one's consecration and the necessity of giving one's obedience to an individual person. In statements which affirm a superior's right to require obedience from one unwilling to give it, CICLSAL may recall that such is to be done either in writing or in the presence of two witnesses. This detail is important if sanctions may follow.

CICLSAL also requires a general norm in the constitutions on the dress of the community accompanied by a descriptive norm in the directives. These norms are often recommended for the topic of consecration or of poverty. The first states that the dress of the community is worn as a sign of consecrated life. The second states the general type of dress.

Prayer, community, ministry, and formation are the fundamental means for consecrated life. Those consecrating their lives receive an assignment in ministry from the superior and live with others of the community in a place designated by the superior. Each community provides itself with times, places, and occasions for eucharistically-oriented participation in the sacraments, in daily communal and individual prayers, and in seasonal or occasional retreats, penances, devotions, and relaxations. These gatherings in Christ recall Christ's communion with the Father and the Spirit and provide opportunities for reconciliation of what is holy with what is not yet whole, of the living with the dead, of those freed in Christ with those not yet freed.

Formation for prayer and ministry as a Christian community begins with admission as a novice under the direction of one appointed by the superior from among the perpetually professed. The one appointed directs all the activities of the novice for at least twelve months in the place designated by the superior as the novitiate. Formation continues with the pronouncement of vows received by the superior.

In the areas of prayer, community, ministry, and formation, CICLSAL emphasizes the practice of daily Eucharist when possible, frequent participation in the sacrament of reconciliation, life in common with others of the community, determination by the superior of one's ministry, and the need for a novice to complete twelve months of formation in the novitiate before admission by the superior to profession of consecrated life in the community.

Consecrated life requires, moreover, the general means for life in community: governance, administration of goods, separations, and obligations to constitutions. Through regular meetings of its governing body, namely its chapter, a community elects from among those perpetually professed its superior. If the constitutions of the community call for the election of councilors, rather than their appointment, the chapter elects a council to assist the superior in matters determined by the constitutions. The superior appoints a treasurer and, assisted by the council, directs the treasurer in the administration of the goods acquired by the community for its ministry. If anyone wishes temporary or permanent separation from the community the superior challenges and assists the individual's choice for transfer to another community, or for exclaustration up to three years, or for dispensation from vows. If someone shows disregard for the obligations assumed through profession, the superior acting collegially with the council may request of the Holy See an imposed exclaustration or dismissal from the community. Everyone in the community assumes the obligations noted in the constitutions. The chapter regularly reviews these and by a two-thirds vote may petition the Holy See for specific changes.

CICLSAL emphasizes that there be specific norms for elections and a specific list of instances which require the superior to have the consent of the council to act. The chapter is a delegate chapter, unless the community's tradition and approved constitutions direct otherwise. Its membership consists of a majority elected by and from those professed in the community. Both the superior and the treasurer report to the chapter on their term of service. After completion of elections and attention to major needs of the community, the chapter is closed. If an interim chapter, known as an extraordinary chapter, is needed, the superior with the consent of the council may convoke it. If the superior dies, resigns, or is incapacitated, the councilor previously elected or designated assumes the role of the superior and convokes a chapter to elect a superior. The chapter and the constitutions may determine further participative organs of the community.

CICLSAL also emphasizes that there be intermediary superiors who are accountable for specific parts and communities. Such superiors may be elected by the part served or by the community served if the constitution does not direct otherwise and if the one elected receives confirmation from the higher superior. Intermediary superiors exercise personal authority in their respective areas.

III. Questions on Church Law

The overall framework of the questions CICLSAL asks is that of faith and the Christian faithful. The documents CICLSAL critiques set forth Christian priorities, which are determined by unceasing reflection on the on-going experience of the life of Christ in the Christian faithful. No individual or community autonomously determines these priorities. They are determined by collaboration in, with, and through Christ.

In the process of determining its priorities, the Church acquires a clearer identity among the churches, nations, and other organizations of the world. Out of this identity the Church speaks the law given it for the sake of humanity. Both the questions asked by CICLSAL and the responses given by the Church's communities of consecrated life contribute significantly to the development and strength of this law.

Margaret Mary Modde, O.S.F.

This article originally appeared in *Bulletin on Issues of Religious Law*, Vol. 1, 1985.

2.
WHAT IS MEANT BY THE "PERSONAL AUTHORITY" OF RELIGIOUS SUPERIORS?

The term "personal authority" is frequently used today in reference to religious superiors. This basic concept of authority attached to an office is not new, but in an era of increased interest in more participative forms of governance, the term is used to distinguish the superior's authority from that exercised by a group.

While the 1917 Code described all religious superiors as having "dominative" power (CIC 503), the parallel canon of the 1983 Code (596, §1) simply states:

> Superiors and chapters of institutes enjoy that power over members which is defined in universal law and the constitutions.

Superiors in clerical religious institutes of pontifical right also possess the ecclesiastical power of governance for both internal and external forums (c. 596, §2). All religious superiors, however, have some share in the ecclesiastical power of governing (c. 596, §3).

As seen above, canon 596, §1 refers to both superiors and chapters. Although, like "personal authority," the words do not appear in the canons, general chapters are said to act "collegially" and are spoken of often as the highest "extraordinary" authority of the congregation. Complementing this collegial, extraordinary authority is the personal and ordinary authority of the superior.

Canons on the ecclesiastical power of governance describe ordinary power as that which is joined to a certain office by the law itself (c. 131, §1). An ecclesiastical office, in turn, is described as a function stably constituted by law, to be exercised for a spiritual purpose. Its obligations and rights are also defined in the law (cf. c. 145). This ordinary power is distinguished from delegated power which is "granted to a person but not by means of an office" (c. 131, §1). Rather it is granted by one who possesses ordinary executive power (cf. c. 137, §1).

The office of religious superior, the source of its authority and its key rights and responsibilities are found primarily in canons 618-619. These are further delineated in each institute's proper law (cf. cc. 596, §1 and 617). The superior's power is "received from God through the ministry of the Church" and must be exercised "in a spirit of service" (c. 618). *Essential Elements* further clarifies the ecclesial mediation of religious authority:

> It is conferred by the Church at the time of establishing each institute and by the approving of its constitutions. It is an authority invested in superiors for the duration of their term of service … (EE 49).

Canon 618 notes that the "superior's authority to decide and prescribe what must be done" remains intact. However, it also requires of the superior docility to the will of God, reverence for the human person, promotion of voluntary obedience, willing listening, and efforts to foster collaboration for the good of the institute and the

Church. A superior's primary obligation is to work toward a true community in Christ, using various means: the Word and sacred liturgy, personal example of virtue and fidelity, and careful attention to individual needs — especially of the sick, the restless, and the faint of heart (cf. c. 619).

To assist them in this role, superiors are required to have councils (c. 627). While certain actions cannot be taken validly by superiors without the advice or consent of this body, many superiors so value this collaboration that they deliberate with their councils much more frequently than is required by law. With this new emphasis on "teams" or "shared decision making" came further clarifications of the superior's personal authority, vis á vis consultative bodies.

Experimentation with governance gave rise to certain concerns. In 1972, a question was submitted to CICLSAL regarding whether or not there could be an exclusive and collegial form of ordinary government for a total religious institute, a province, or an individual house so that the superior, if any, was merely an executor. The response, based on *Perfectae caritatis* 14 and *Evangelica testificatio* 15, was negative. The brief response stated that the superior must have "personal authority" with consideration for legitimate consultation and limitations according to common and particular law. *Essential Elements* cites the same sources when calling for "effective, personal religious authority" at all levels. This is so that religious obedience can be lived (EE 52).

Recognition of personal authority acknowledges that obedience, as such, is not to a group. Nevertheless, in the spirit of obedience, members will cooperate in implementing legitimately made corporate decisions, as well as those of a superior. Personal authority also respects the privacy of an individual, providing for confidentiality in personal difficulties.

What is being asked of congregations, as they submit constitutions for approbation, is not a highly authoritarian description of the superior's office, but rather one in which two dimensions are balanced: 1) personal authority, exercised according to universal and proper law by those in office; and 2) responsibility for the good of the whole, shared by all members.

In this context, it is helpful to recall the broad purpose of religious government: "The building of a united community in Christ in which God is sought and loved before all things, and the mission of Christ is generously accomplished" (EE 51). All members share in this pursuit of communion and mission. A diversity of functions as well as gifts can facilitate collaboration.

Noting that personal authority cannot actually be shared, except by delegation, Hill notes, "The skill again lies in the ability to delegate and to work cooperatively with others." The office of religious superior and its obligations and rights constitute the personal authority of the individual holding office. There remains great latitude for collaboration.

Sharon Holland, I.H.M.

This article originally appeared in *Bulletin on Issues of Religious Law*, Vol. 1, 1985.

3.
CAN A RELIGIOUS INSTITUTE ADOPT A COLLEGIAL FORM OF GOVERNMENT?

The question itself reveals some of the complexities and underlying issues in governance for religious today. The obvious answer to the question is in the affirmative, since both the Benedictine and Dominican traditions have, from the very beginning, incorporated a collegial form of government. But having said that, I do not believe that I have answered the intent of the question; so please let me clarify.

The basic model of authority in the code is that of a person who, by virtue of an office or position, has authority over other people. That person in office may or may not be required to have a council or body of consultors, and there are situations where the person may be required to seek the advice or consent of this body of consultors or council. In religious life, this person is usually known by the title of superior, and the emphasis or stress in replies from CICLSAL has been on the personal authority of the superior to act. In situations where the superior interacts with his or her "subjects," the canons are clear to point out that the superior's ability to make the decision remains intact (e.g., c. 618).

Recent church documents such as *Mutual Relations* (nn. 42 and 49) emphasize that there is no sharing of religious authority and that religious authority comes from its conferral by the appropriate church authorities. What is at issue today is whether or not collegiality and other interpretations of the exercise of authority and obedience within a religious institute are possible. J. M. R. Tillard, in his book, *A Gospel Path*, emphasizes that the type of authority adopted in a religious institute is one of its essential traits, but that often the social context exercises considerable influence on this choice and, in some cases, the model of authority adopted is that proposed by either custom or Roman norms. In contrast, canon 578 of the new code speaks about the patrimony of an institute, including the intentions of the founders and all that is approved regarding the nature, purpose, spirit and character of the institute and its traditions, as well as the true autonomy of life, particularly of governance, which is mentioned in canon 586 for each institute. The previous code of canon law presumed one basic model for the exercise of authority in religious life. This model was focused on superiors whose authority was conditioned by the seeking of advice or consent from their council. What is at issue is whether or not that model remains normative and the only acceptable model for the exercise of governance within religious institutes today. The question itself sometimes evokes much emotional reaction when presumptions are made about the various theologies of religious life, particularly the understanding of the vow of obedience.

With regard to the specific form of government, religious institutes must be true to the tradition and spirituality from which they spring. No religious institute can forget that its origin is in the Holy Spirit and its object is the following of Christ. Within the monastic tradition, the collegial form of government is basically normative. While St. Benedict vested authority in the abbot, he also sought to insure that all major matters were brought before the community as a whole in chapter. While in chapter, the community is operating in a collegial form of government, since all members of chapter participate as a body with equal voice and vote. Within the Dominican tradition, chapter holds a place of honor, as well as a primary place in Dominican identity and governance. Therefore, as with Benedictines, the use of chapters by Dominicans as a collegial form of governance is soundly rooted in the traditions and is an operative model for government. Within apostolic communities and those communities which can identify no specific tradition, the use of superiors to facilitate ministry and internal organization, as well as to focus the nature and exercise of the vow of obedience, seems to have been the historical development. There is no doubt but that collegial forms of government are very much a part of the history of religious life; the question today seems to be whether or not they can be seen as supplementary to the basic model of superior (and council) or as a totally distinct model.

Other than the individual question of the exercise of authority, the 1983 Code also looks to values which must be protected and exercised for the common good of the community. These values are mentioned in a number of places, but particularly in canon 602, which talks about the family life of an institute, and canons 618 and 619, which list duties assigned to the superiors. Whether or not someone holds the title of superior, these concerns must be noted for the good of the community.

On the highest level of the institute (known as the general level for apostolic institutes and usually the priory level for those of the monastic and mendicant traditions), the code sees the usual (i.e., day-to-day) functioning of governance as being vested in a superior, who is called the supreme moderator, assisted by a council. The advice or consent of this council is to be utilized as required either by the code or by the particular law of the institute. The only place where a collegial vote of the superior and council is called for by the code is in canon 699 — on the dismissal of members. Canon 627 requires that all superiors have a council, in accord with the particular law of the institute, and that they use it in the exercise of their office. It is left to the particular law of an institute to determine when advice or consent of that council must be sought, other than those cases required by the code. On levels below the general level then, there is usually an intermediate level and a local level. The intermediate level usually operates in an analogous fashion to the general level. On the local level, the superior may be resident or non-resident, and often the members of the local community (when this community is not too numerous) function in a collegial fashion in making their decisions. Depending on one's tradition, this use of the local community operating in a collegial fashion is seen either as a local council or a local chapter.

In summary then, religious institutes employ a collegial form of government whenever they use chapters or whenever particular local houses function as a group in decision-making. In other instances, I believe that the religious institute can certainly adopt a collegial form of governance in any instance where the law (either the code or particular law) does not require the superior to act either alone or with the advice or consent of the council. Since those situations are minimal, there is no restriction on the use of a consensus or collegial form of government in other instances. The canonical concern would be that, when a group is acting in a collegial mode, it be understood that they may not restrict or interfere with the superior's legitimate right to act in the fulfillment of the duties of his/her office. Within the present situation a person must be designated superior at each of the levels mentioned above and he/she must function with the advice or consent of his/her council when required.

The option discussed in some communities within the United States is that of "team" ministry. That option is not available under the current code. The values behind it have been elaborated above, as well as the concern that the respect for the individual religious, the ability to relate and to have one's personal matters protected by confidentiality, require the need to relate to one person rather than to a group. While a superior and council may in one sense function as a "team" in those areas not required by law, even there the specification of tasks is combined with the necessary leadership function and this should be clearly understood by the community whose common good is a primary concern of the law.

Ellen O'Hara, C.S.J.

This article originally appeared in *Bulletin on Issues of Religious Law*, Vol. 1, 1985.

4.
Is it Permissible to Have Direct Election (Non-Chapter) of Supreme Moderators and Major Superiors?

The election of major superiors is covered by canon 631, which specifies that it is normally a function of the general chapter to elect a supreme moderator. Canon 625, §1 indicates that the supreme moderator is to be elected by a canonical election, according to the constitutions. The reference to canonical elections means that canons 164-179 apply, unless particular law provides otherwise. The clause "unless particular law provides otherwise" is important, because it does allow for variations. In answering this question, the election of the supreme moderator or highest internal superior is significantly different from that of other superiors and so will be treated first. Since 1969, the *Canon Law Digest* has published replies from the Congregation for Institutes of Consecrated Life and Societies of Apostolic Life (CICLSAL) to religious communities who have asked about the question of the direct election of the supreme moderator. Although these replies are private and therefore have no legal weight, it is interesting to notice the development of thought. In the earliest replies, the answer is most clearly negative. It is seen to be neither "fitting nor prudent" that the superior general be elected by direct election. Beginning in 1972 and continuing to the present, there has been indication of exceptions being granted, although with the weight of opinion still being in favor of chapter election. It is clear from these replies, as well as from the experience of various religious institutes, that direct election of the supreme moderator may occur. Prior to the promulgation of the 1983 code, the indult from CICLSAL was required in order to effect such a direct election. Since then, the approval of particular law of an institute is sufficient to make allowances for this direct election. Aside from those cases where the Congregation for the Evangelization of Peoples is also required to be involved, the competent authority for the approval of the constitutions of an institute is the diocesan bishop for a diocesan institute and CICLSAL for pontifical institutes. Approval of the particular law of an institute where provision is made for direct election of the supreme moderator has occurred and is therefore obviously legally permissible.

The factors which influence the decision for the direct election of the superior reflect the concerns of the CICLSAL, and the factors appear to be these:

1. There should be no appearance of political maneuvering either for oneself or for someone else;

2. The possibility of polarization, factions, or campaigning should be avoided;

3. The group should be small enough and in sufficient overall contact that the members of the institute know each other well enough;

4. The direct election occurs in such a way that the community can convene in an atmosphere of prayer and spiritual discernment.

Geographical concentration of the members, the size of the community, the avoidance of politicking, and other factors, particularly the customs and traditions of the community, are all relevant in making this decision.

By definition of canon 620, the supreme moderator and her assistant or vicar are considered major superiors. In religious institutes which have various levels of authority, there may be other major superiors (often termed provincials or regionals). The election of these other major superiors is governed by canon 625, §3, which states that the constitutions of the religious institute should state how these major superiors are selected. If they are elected, they require confirmation of the supreme moderator, and if appointed, suitable consultation should precede the appointment. Therefore, the direct election of provincials and their assistants is certainly permissible in the 1983 Code of canon Law. Whether or not such is a good idea depends upon other human factors, such as the traditions of the community and the wishes of the members as reflected in the particular law of the institute.

The issue of who may vote in the direct election of major superiors is sometimes raised. Technically, the question of who has active and passive voice is a matter of particular law of the institute. In some institutes, there is a custom that only perpetually professed may be members of chapter or have active and passive voice; in other communities, temporary professed also exercise active and passive voice if they meet the other requirements of law. In the question of the direct election of a major superior, CICLSAL has indicated at times a preference that this be restricted to the vote of perpetually professed, but this is not a requirement of the code. Another issue which is sometimes raised is the question of votes by mail or by proxy. Canon 167, §1 states that this matter should be determined in particular law. If the particular law of an institute is silent on these issues, mail ballots and proxy votes are not allowed.

Ellen O'Hara, C.S.J.

This article originally appeared in *Bulletin on Issues of Religious Law* Vol. 1, 1985.

5.
ELECTION OF MAJOR SUPERIORS

INTRODUCTION

Major superiors, as designated office-holders in religious institutes, bear responsibility for both spiritual and temporal leadership of the corporate body, the religious community. Because of the pivotal role major superiors have in the life of the institute, and because of the authority and power vested in those who hold such office, the acquisition and exercise of this office is guided by some clear, if general, directives in the Code of Canon Law and by more specific, supplementary legislation in the proper law of the institute.

The term major superior includes not only those who govern the whole institute, but also superiors who govern a province of the institute or the equivalent of a province; those who govern an autonomous house; and the vicars of all of these persons. The code uses the term supreme moderator for those who govern the whole institute; most institutes, drawing upon the traditions of the institute and the cultures from which they spring, use other titles such as superior general, president, minister general, or prioress general. Major superiors other than the supreme moderator likewise have titles which reflect the diverse traditions of religious institutes, e.g., sector superior, regional president, prior provincial, and the like.

This article will focus upon the most common mode by which the office is acquired, that of election. It will review the general parameters within which such elections take place, probe some of the values in tension prior to and during the election process, and address some questions which have been raised in connection with the election of a major superior.

I. GENERAL NOTIONS

While the code gives general directives, it is the proper law of the institute which has the defining role and gives the particular character and shape to the election of major superiors in each institute. The proper law of the institute includes the constitution and the secondary text, often called the directory, as well as other enactments of chapters. What has been determined in the constitution of the institute and approved by the competent authority is the first source to approach when reflecting upon election of a major superior. For instance, while the code requires that the supreme moderator of the institute be designated by canonical election, the same canon states that this election is to be carried out according to the norm of the constitution. Another example of the defining role of the proper law of the institute concerns the election of the superior of an autonomous monastery and of the supreme moderator of an institute of diocesan right. In these elections, there is the additional requirement that the bishop of the diocese preside personally or through a delegate. The code, however, no longer gives the presiding bishop discretionary power to nullify or ratify these elections. If such discretionary power were to be accorded, it now would have to come from the proper law of the institute itself.

For major superiors other than the supreme moderator (i.e., provincial superior, regional president, and the like) the code simply states that they are to be designated according to the norm of the constitution, providing that the following general directives are met: 1) if they are elected, they need confirmation by the highest superior in the institute; and 2) if they are appointed, some appropriate consultation should precede the appointment.

Aside from the directives cited above and contained in the code, it is the proper law of the institute which determines the particulars regarding the election of major superior, such as the length of term for the office, some of the qualifications necessary to be eligible for office, the size and composition of the electoral body, the manner of balloting, and the like. When the matter concerns the election of the highest superior or supreme moderator, some of these particulars (e.g., length of term) must be in the constitution. Although canonical requirements such as those contained in canons 169-172 are binding, some other norms of the code may be modified by the constitutions. When the matter concerns the election of other major superiors, the particulars may be found in other parts of the proper law (e.g., the directory or provincial statutes).

II. Underlying Values

During an era of change such as that being experienced by religious institutes in the United States, little within religious life is left unquestioned. The manner in which the institute selects its leadership is subject to scrutiny as the institute tests the compatibility of the process with the institute's self-understanding. Before addressing some of the particular questions raised in connection with the election of a major superior, it might be helpful to identify some of the underlying values to which the questions speak.

Stability and change are two values in tension at the time of an election for major superior. The election of a major superior sometimes introduces a period of uncertainty, and perhaps even organizational unrest, within a religious institute. This may be true, although to a lesser degree, even when the incumbent is eligible for and seems assured of re-election. Those who hold office in a religious institute, as well as the various structures and processes by which an institute conducts its internal business, should always have in view the good of the institute. So, too, the processes by which leadership is selected should contribute to the good of the institute, both its present peace and effectiveness and its ability to incorporate the demands of the future. Because of the uncertainty accompanying the selection of leadership, it is desirable that the process itself be a stabilizing element rather than a divisive element, and that it be understood and accepted by the membership, thereby contributing to the institute's sense of order and well-being.

Openness and confidentiality, although not necessarily in opposition with each other, are also values in tension at the time of the election of the major superior. In the United States, leaders of many religious institutes have modeled a high degree of openness in financial accountability, internal consultation prior to direction-setting or decision-making, and regular communication regarding major projects, congregational ministries, and activities of members. Such openness has resulted in high levels of participation and a sense of ownership by the members. It is natural for members to transfer similar expectations to the processes through which leadership is selected. The expectation of participating in such an important matter as the selection of leadership is also in keeping with the ancient and respected jurisprudential principle which urges the approval of all in matters which affect all, a concept presently found in canon 119 of the code.

Related to the openness/confidentiality tension are concomitant concerns for the freedom of the electors and the reputations of those being considered for office. Expressed negatively the guiding questions might be: What kinds of conduct are prejudicial to freedom? What are harmful to persons?

Expectations of openness and involvement, when translated into specific actions or activities, can lead to some conflict in a canonical election because of some of the protections built into the canonical election process. Canonical election requires that for a vote to be valid, it must be secret. The primary reason for requiring a secret vote is to preserve the freedom of the electors. This requirement functions as a deterrent to the many types of pressure to which electors could be subject. The requirement of secrecy refers to the act of voting itself and not to what an elector might reveal prior to or subsequent to casting a vote. However, for an elector to reveal her or his choice is at least imprudent. Certain participatory processes preliminary to the actual balloting which require participation by the electors could infringe upon the secrecy to which the elector is bound.

On the other hand, the voters have an obligation to inform themselves regarding the character and qualifications of the various candidates prior to casting their ballots. In smaller religious institutes, ordinary interaction around the internal business of the community might well be the means of obtaining the necessary knowledge. Other more formal vehicles may also be provided for ascertaining the necessary knowledge for those who wish to make use of them. These might include open forums, interviews (oral, published, or video-taped) and the circulation of vitae. Such processes have often proved helpful, particularly in larger religious institutes and those spread over a wide geographic area. It is also important to ascertain, however, that any processes reflect the will of the institute, not just that of one culture or language group or of a small subgroup of the institute. In other words, there needs to be a "fit" between these preliminary processes and the institute itself.

Whatever vehicles of communication a particular religious institute chooses, they must be shaped and carried out so that their purpose — the exchange of information — is clear. If processes conducted under the aegis of the institute, or even private discussions, cross over from being information exchange to persuasion, they are no longer assisting the electors but may be prejudicing the election. Procuring of votes, whether done directly or indirectly, for oneself or for another, is to be avoided.

In tension with the electors' need for knowledge is the right of each person, prospective candidate or not, to her or his good name and to appropriate privacy. The decision by the leadership of the religious institute that some form of preliminary process would benefit the institute as a whole may result in exerting pressure upon potential candidates to participate or to justify their non-participation. Therefore, any information exchange process should be conducted with great sensitivity to the persons involved, graciously acknowledging their right to participate or not and assiduously protecting each person's right to a good name. Despite the heightened degree of "public" scrutiny which naturally accompanies such processes, the spirit of charity should be palpable as the institute begins to identify its future leaders.

Finally, the election of a major superior, whatever the particulars, is a religious act in which the participants, conscious of God's pervasive presence in human history, freely and responsibly elect those whom they believe to be worthy and suitable. Carried out in this spirit, the election itself becomes an act of worship of God and a means of expressing truth, witnessing to unity, and participating in the construction of the future. This understanding of election as religious act is made explicit by the prayerful context, the reverence for persons, and the peaceful and respectful atmosphere in which the election is conducted. Each religious institute will enflesh these elements differently, but each must be attentive to them, thereby providing the conditions in which the election of the major superior may be more than a juridical or political act.

III. Particular Questions and Special Circumstances

Having probed some of the values held in balance at the time of the election of a major superior, we turn now to some of the particular questions which have been raised around this topic.

Despite the clarity of certain provisions in the code regarding some matters and the discretion accorded individual religious institutes to establish in their proper law provision for other matters, questions often arise regarding the election of major superiors. The questions surface for a variety of reasons. These reasons include silence in the proper law on a particular issue, insufficient experience on the part of those charged with preparing for the election process, or radically-changed circumstances within the institute, such as a significant fluctuation in number of members, major shift in geographic distribution of members, or access to new modes of communication, to name a few. Changed circumstances within the institute may pose possibilities or problems which had not been dealt with in the recent history of the institute.

A. Preliminary Processes

Each religious institute and/or province prepares for the election of the major superior; this preparation is both remote and proximate. Such preparation may include the convoking of a chapter by the incumbent major superior; a call to prayer on the part of the entire institute, province, or region; and the establishment of a committee to attend to various organizational matters. The proper law of some religious institutes specifies quite clearly what preliminary processes or consultations are to be conducted. Some designate a straw ballot, a consultative vote, or a nomination process involving all the members of the institute or province. This can be a helpful vehicle for ascertaining a sense of the province or institute-at-large, and could be decisive for some electors. However, it is important to point out that the electors are not bound by the slate or terna except in the unusual case where the proper law of the institute explicitly states that they are so bound. Each elector has both the right and the responsibility to cast his or her ballot for the person whom he or she considers most suitable, and the free exercise of this right may not be restricted lightly.

B. Discernment

Increasingly, religious institutes in the United States speak of a desire to discern as a body. Such a movement is in keeping with the understanding that this important action in the life of the institute is a religious act. The term discernment, however, carries different meanings, ranging from the very broad and referring to a general disposition or climate, to the more specific, referring to particular activities and expectations.

Discernment in its broad sense, understood as prayerful reflection on a human situation in the light of faith, is the ordinary approach of religious persons to the important decisions of their lives. Such reflection becomes more truly discernment as the individual becomes more attuned to God's presence. Certain specific manifestations of communal discernment which require group discussions of positive and negative aspects of potential candidates, open airing of differing opinions, and structured movement toward agreement can be difficult to reconcile with the requirement that the vote of each elector be free and secret. In addition to concern for the freedom of the electors, there is also concern that "public" discussions of persons could be harmful to them. Therefore, any group discernment process prior to a canonical election that places pressure on electors to violate their right and obligation of secrecy or which impairs the freedom of the act of election is incompatible with the values which a canonical election process seeks, with good reason, to protect. In addition, attempts to substitute the group discernment process for the election is likewise incompatible.

C. Universal Suffrage

Universal suffrage is a mode of election in which every member of the body who is professed the required number of years has the right to cast a ballot. In some religious institutes, universal suffrage traces its origin to the founding charism and has been confirmed by centuries-long custom. Institutes with such traditions are usually monastic institutes. Other institutes, small in size, also elect the major superior by universal suffrage. In still other institutes, the highest superior is designated by canonical election, as required by the code, but other major superiors are elected by universal suffrage in the province or region, according to the proper law of the institute.

In recent years in the United States some religious institutes, with neither a long-standing custom nor a small number of members, have considered the possibility of universal suffrage, seeing it as a more appropriate process for electing the major superior. Such consideration builds on the desire and expectation that all members be involved in matters of major concern in the institute, incorporating some of the positive values of United States cultures. Some of these religious institutes have sought a change in or dispensation from their constitution in order to allow for universal suffrage in the election of the highest superior. Requests for such changes or dispensations have regularly been denied by the Congregation of Institutes of Consecrated Life and Societies of Apostolic Life (CICLSAL) when the requesting institute numbered more than 100 members. Reasons cited in the response usually include some of the following: inadequate knowledge about likely candidates on the part of all members; the possibility of factions emerging within the institute or of campaigning; concern about the prayerful atmosphere and religious nature of the election; and the convergence of insight which is perceived to be more likely in a delegate chapter. An additional practical concern about universal suffrage, one not mentioned in the CICLSAL responses, is the potential impact of an increasing number of elderly voters as the demographics of many religious institutes in the United States change.

The requirement that the highest superior be designated by canonical election (c. 626), is the norm for religious institutes. The process by which other major superiors are designated remains a matter of proper law.

D. POSTULATION

At the time of election of the major superior, a religious institute may find itself in the position of wishing to vote for a member of the institute who is not eligible for the office. If the prospective candidate is otherwise suitable but is ineligible by reason of an impediment which can be, and frequently is, dispensed, it may be possible for the electoral body to propose such a candidate through postulation.

By the process of postulation the electors propose a candidate to the competent authority, who may either admit the candidate or decline to do so. In the case of postulation for the office of supreme moderator of a pontifical institute, the competent authority is CICLSAL. For the supreme moderator of an institute of diocesan right and of some autonomous monasteries, the competent authority is the diocesan bishop. In the case of postulation of a provincial or regional superior of a pontifical institute, proper law may provide that the competent authority be the supreme moderator of the institute, but if the proper law is silent on the matter the competent authority is CICLSAL. For a provincial or regional superior of a diocesan institute the competent authority is the diocesan bishop.

The general law of the Church allows for postulation whenever a canonical election is called for, and a religious institute may make use of this provision unless its own proper law expressly prohibits it. In the event that the electing body postulates a candidate for office and the competent authority declines to admit the person postulated, the right of election reverts to the electoral body.

The process of postulating a candidate, although a rather simple one, has some quite specific requirements. Among these are: the stipulation that the electors must indicate on their ballots that they are postulating, rather than electing, a candidate; a two-thirds vote of the electing body is required for a postulation to have effect, regardless of the ordinary election procedures of the institutes; certain other specifics for confirmation, dispensation from the impediment, and acceptance of the office must be followed carefully. Canons 180-184 in the code offer guidance in the process of postulation.

The more stringent requirements for postulation as compared with election suggest that postulation is not favored but rather permitted in extraordinary circumstances. Postulation is a provision for seeking a dispensation from the law, and requires sufficient cause in order to be granted. Because many former impediments are no longer included in the present code or in revised constitutions, the most common circumstances in which religious institutes today have recourse to this provision are: 1) the desire to elect the major superior for an additional term of office beyond what is permitted by the constitution of the institute; or 2) the desire to elect a major superior who has not yet fulfilled the requisite years in perpetual or definitive profession as specified in the proper law of the institute. Smaller institutes and autonomous monasteries are more apt to find themselves in these circumstances than larger institutes. Informal surveys suggest that the competent authority to admit the postulation, given sufficient cause, is usually willing to do so once, but only rarely a second time. A common exception to this one-time admission practice seems to be the response to postulation for the founders of institutes, where the benefits of preserving the formative spirit of the founder and avoiding the divisions often experienced in a young community outweigh other values.

It may be of some comfort or interest to know that postulating a candidate for an additional term as major superior is not a contemporary phenomenon alone. On March 2, 1920 the Sacred Congregation for Religious (a predecessor to CICLSAL) circulated a letter remarking on the excessive number of such requests and reminding religious institutes that the simple desire of the voters or the fitness of the person postulated was not by itself sufficient reason for the postulation.

From the above discussion it can be seen that the clear preference of the church, found both in law and practice, is that the office of major superior be a temporary one, filled for a definite and limited time and then turned over to a successor. Most major superiors and members alike agree that this is usually in the best interest of both the office holder and the institute itself. Such consensus, confirmed by experience, suggests there might be wisdom in limited tenure for other ecclesiastical offices also.

E. INCOMPLETE TERM

Some religious institutes find themselves with a vacancy in the office of major superior at a time other than at the end of a term. This could happen due to the death, incapacity, resignation, or removal of the incumbent. The general law of the church indicates that any such vacancy should be filled within three months from the time of notice of the vacancy unless the proper law provides otherwise. Once again, even in the unusual circumstance of an incomplete term, the particular law of the institute takes precedence over the general law. The constitution of each institute should provide for emergency succession and give direction for a special election such as this. Frequently, if there is a relatively short period of time remaining in the incumbent's term, e.g., a year or less, the constitution directs that the vicar (i.e., assistant general superior, vicar provincial, and the like) complete the term, thus avoiding the time, planning, and expense of another election.

In times of change such as religious institutes in the United States are experiencing now, some institutes are choosing to realign themselves through mergers or unions. The term merger usually connotes one unit joining another, in the process losing its own identity; in a union, the units both (or all) lose their former identities and a new entity comes into being. These structural changes may involve units within an institute (provinces, regions) or two or more institutes themselves. The timing of these structural changes does not always coincide with the terms of the major superiors affected. The extensive planning undertaken preparatory to change on this scale should include provision for the manner and timing of the selection of leadership for the new entity(-ies), as well as provision for the transition period itself. Mergers and unions of institutes are reserved to the Holy See. Therefore, the nature of the new entity and all the constitutive elements of government, including provision for leadership, would be included in the proposal submitted to CICLSAL. Restructuring of parts within an institute is carried out by the institute itself following the norms of its constitution. In either situation it is not unusual for the term of major superiors to be interrupted before completion or for the manner of selection of the major superior to be altered.

F. NON-ACCEPTANCE OF ELECTION

It has happened that a religious institute has elected as major superior a person who does not feel suited or called to serve in this capacity. In a canonical election, the person elected does not assume office until the election has been accepted and, if confirmation is required, until it has been confirmed. The person elected is free to accept or decline the office. Ordinarily this occurs immediately, and such alacrity would seem to be in the best interest of the institute. However, unless the proper law of the institute states otherwise, the person elected has eight days after being notified of her or his election to make the decision to accept or decline the office. If the decision is to decline the office, another election takes place.

Conclusion

The office of major superior, like that of all superiors in religious institutes, exists for the good of the institute and of the Church. For the majority of religious institutes in the United States, the major superiors are designated through canonical election. The canonical election process, like any election, is premised on the freedom of the electors to choose. Certain aspects of the canonical election process are specified in detail to insure that the outcome of the election is beyond question, thus providing for an orderly and peaceful continuation or transfer of leadership. The electors, through their individual, informed choices, assure the quality and suitability of those elected. And it is the members of the religious institute themselves who, through fidelity to their charism and mission and through the quality of their life together, make possible and encourage members in their full development as persons, thus assuring leaders for the future.

Rosemary Smith, S.C.

This article originally appeared in *Bulletin on Issues of Religious Law*, Vol. 8, 1992.

6.
LAITY AND THE POWER OF GOVERNANCE: A STATEMENT OF THE QUESTION

A Statement of the Question

With increasing frequency today, one hears questions about the exercise of governing power by lay persons in the Church. Among these are questions of particular relevance for lay religious. For example:

What is the nature of the authority exercised by lay religious superiors?

What powers can be delegated to a lay chancellor, or to a sister or brother serving in an office for religious?

Can a brother be elected superior in a clerical institute?

Under the 1917 Code of Canon Law, these and similar questions had clear negative answers. During the code revision process however, there emerged a decisive movement away from the prohibitions of the past. Today, although much remains to be done through serious research by canonists and theologians, it is possible to attempt at least a "current state of the question" on what is sometimes called "lay jurisdiction."

In the 1917 Code, only clerics could obtain the power of orders or of jurisdiction (c. 118). The various degrees of power of orders were obtained through ordination and the degrees of jurisdiction, for all but the Supreme Pontiff, were received by canonical appointment (c. 109). Ecclesiastical offices, by strict definition, involved some participation in ecclesiastical power — either of orders or jurisdiction (c. 145). The power of jurisdiction was equated with power of governing (*iurisdictionis seu regiminis*, c. 196) and ordinary power of governance was that attached ipso iure to an office (c. 197).

Within this legal system it was clear that only clerics exercised the power of ecclesiastical governance and did so within various stably constituted offices reserved to them. Consequently it is not surprising that only clerical exempt religious superiors were described as possessing ecclesiastical power of jurisdiction for both the internal and the external forum. All other religious superiors exercised "dominative" power (c. 501). The position of a lay superior could not be called an ecclesiastical office because such an office included participation in the power of governance which was reserved to clerics.

Also of significance in the 1917 Code was the division of ecclesiastical power into the power of orders and the power of governance. Although both could be exercised only by clerics, the two were seen as flowing from distinct sources: ordination and canonical mission.

During the code revision process, it appeared that this two-fold source of the power of governance had opened the way for lay participation in the exercise of that power. A significant step had already been taken by Pope Paul VI when he authorized the use of lay judges in collegiate tribunals. This was viewed by many canonists, though not all, as a clear example of lay persons exercising the power of governance. By the time of the 1981 plenarium of the code commission, in which the revised canons would undergo final scrutiny before being submitted to Pope John Paul II, there were important new versions of some canonical texts.

A norm which combined concepts from canons 196 and 118 of the 1917 Code included a new openness to lay participation in the power of governance. The text acknowledged the divine institution of the power of governance (*potestas regiminis*) in the church which, it noted, was also called power of jurisdiction (*potestas iurisdictionis*). Those in sacred orders were able to possess that power. In addition however:

> ... insofar as it does not depend on sacred orders, the lay Christian faithful may have that part in the exercise of this power which is conceded to them in particular cases by the supreme authority of the Church.

In this text then, clerics were, by their state, capable of possessing the power of governance; laity might have a part in its exercise by special concession of the Church's highest authority, and in matters not requiring the power of orders. The latter seemed precisely what Paul VI had done in the case of lay judges.

Within the context of a new broader definition of ecclesiastical office, a draft canon made distinctions regarding office holders. It stated that only clerics could hold offices which required the power of orders or the ecclesiastical power of governance dependent on orders (*ordine sacro innixa*).

These changes in the law raised the obvious problem of discerning which offices and exercises of the power of governance were dependent upon the power of orders. The use of lay judges seemed to identify one office which did not require orders. On the other hand, the canons made clear that offices involving the full care of souls, such as the office of pastor, must be filled by a priest. Between these two, many areas would have to be sorted out. Nevertheless, it seemed from the schema that a real exercise of the ecclesiastical power of governance by lay persons was envisioned.

As preparations for the above-mentioned 1981 plenarium progressed, these canons and the questions surrounding them emerged as one of six special questions to be discussed. Some objected to the new texts on two grounds: a) they introduced a distinction between power of governance dependent upon orders and that not dependent on orders; and b) they admit lay persons to the exercise of the latter. They proposed the removal of this distinction and the suppression of the canon which provided for lay collegiate judges.

This point of view was based on a perception of Vatican II as teaching a unity of sacred power entirely sourced in sacred orders. While this argumentation was not accepted by a majority of those preparing the plenarium, it was put forward for consideration by all. But plenarium members were also reminded of a 1977 Congregation for the Doctrine of the Faith opinion which included the statement that dogmatically, laity are excluded only from intrinsically hierarchical offices. Papers prepared by selected experts revealed the complexity of the matter.

In a much simpler way, Cardinal Freeman of Sydney verbalized the concerns of some. He observed that the canons illustrate the fact that the exact nature of power in the church has not been clarified. He saw unnecessary confusion in the identification of *potestas regiminis* with *potestas iurisdictionis*. Canonical exactness, he argued, favors a single term for a single concept. It would be preferable to reserve jurisdiction to the judicial field. Then he continued:

> A participation in the exercitium of a *potestas* without holding the power is a new invention which creates its own problems.
>
> A *"potestas regiminis in ordine sacro non innixa"* is a dangerous concept. Where does such a power come from?
>
> Further study needs to be done. The new code can only make sure that the way is left open for this study.

The fundamental question placed before the plenarium was whether or not to retain those canons which recognized that the supreme authority of the church could concede to lay persons some participation in the exercise of the power of governance not dependent on sacred orders. The final vote was decisively in favor of retaining the canons.

In a final revision of the texts, direct reference to a power of governance not dependent on orders was omitted. Canon 129 now speaks of a *potestas regiminis* which is also called *potestas iurisdictionis*. Those in sacred orders may possess it. The canon's second article then adds:

> Lay members of the Christian faithful can cooperate in the exercise of this power in accord with the norm of law.

The norms of the code do provide for many offices previously reserved to clerics to be held by lay persons.

The Code of Canons of the Eastern Churches (1990) provides the same legislation but its parallel canon 979, §1, does not contain the phrase *et etiam potestas iurisdictionis vocatur*. Actually the Latin code itself makes little use of the actual term jurisdiction. Following the above use in canon 129, §1, the word appears another four times in Book VII.

Turning specifically to religious, the code's new description of office in canon 145, §1 is easily applicable to the role of religious superiors.

> An ecclesiastical office is any function constituted in a stable manner by divine or ecclesiastical law to be exercised for a spiritual purpose.

As has been observed, the text prescinds from the question of offices necessarily involving ecclesiastical power of orders or of governance.

In treating the power involved in the office of religious superior, the canons on institutes of consecrated life no longer use the term "dominative" power. Canon 596, §1 simply states that superiors possess the power defined in universal law and constitutions. The canon's second article attributes to superiors of pontifical, clerical religious institutes the ecclesiastical power of governance for both the internal and external forum.

The final article of canon 596 states:

> The prescriptions of canons 131; 133; and 137-144 are applicable to the power referred to in n.1.

As noted, the power referred to in canon 596, §1 is not defined. The canons applied to it, however, are all taken from the section of the code on the ecclesiastical power of governance.

A review of the plenarium reports indicates a conviction that lay superiors exercise some form of public ecclesiastical power, even if all were not of a mind to identify that with the *potestas regiminis*. That lay superiors exercise public power in the church is surely supported canonically by: a) the omission of the term "dominative" power, which was understood as private, b) a definition of office which embraces the role of all religious superiors, c) the provisions of canon 129, §2 for lay participation in the ecclesiastical power of governance, and d) the application of canons from the power of governance to the power common to all religious superiors. Among the canons not applied to all superiors is canon 134, which includes the major superiors of clerical pontifical religious institutes among those known as "ordinaries" in the church.

In an extensive study of the question, G. Ghirlanda concludes that since power in the church is one, power in institutes of consecrated life and societies is of the same nature as the ecclesiastical power of governance. In the case of lay religious institutes (or diocesan clerical institutes) this is conferred *ipso iure* by the code.

While there still must be extensive study of these questions, the very context of the canons on ecclesiastical power of governance signals that there has been a significant change. The parallel texts of the 1917 code were in Book II's treatment of clerics; in the 1983 Code, these canons are in Book I on general norms. By removal of reference to the power of governance dependent on orders, the law avoided canonizing a theological statement which remains open to further study. In the meantime, the revision of the canons, based on the teachings of Vatican II, has opened new doors for lay participation in the life of the Church and its governance.

NEW OPPORTUNITIES

Evidence of some of these new opportunities is seen in the increased frequency with which lay persons — especially religious brothers and sisters — are serving as diocesan chancellors and tribunal officials. The canons provide for this explicitly. However, other questions have quickly arisen: Can these persons be delegated further powers, such as granting dispensations? Bishops are accustomed to giving such delegation to priests; they now ask how much they may delegate to lay officials.

Canonists present diverse views on this question. Certain considerations may be set forth toward reaching a conclusion:

1. Dispensation from merely ecclesiastical law is an act of executive power which can be delegated (c. 85).

2. Ordinary executive power can be delegated for a single act or for all cases, unless the law provides to the contrary (c. 137, §1).

3. The canons do not delineate to whom power may be delegated nor do they state any prohibition against delegation to certain persons.

4. The 1983 Code no longer restricts all power of governance to clerics, but provides for lay persons to cooperate in its exercise (c. 129, §2).

In view of this, it would seem, for example, that the power to dispense from unreserved impediments to marriage which are of ecclesiastical law could be delegated by the local ordinary to a lay chancellor or tribunal official. For practical purposes, this would most frequently be a question of disparity of cult and dispensation from canonical form. Similarly, it would seem that such persons could also be authorized to grant the permission necessary for mixed marriages. Obviously if an individual delegated such powers does not have formal canonical training, adequate preparation for handling the matters delegated will be essential.

Following a similar line of reasoning, it would seem that a religious brother or sister serving in place of an episcopal vicar for religious could be delegated or mandated to fulfill certain functions assigned, by law, to the ordinary or the diocesan bishop personally. While the law reserves the office of episcopal vicar to priests (c. 478), many of the services of a diocesan office for religious do not require sacred orders or ordinary power of governance. A typical example of a matter which is assigned by law to the bishop is presiding at the elections of the superior of an autonomous monastery or of the general superior of a diocesan institute. Since superiors of pontifical institutes of brothers and sisters preside at their own elections, it is clear that lay religious may serve in this capacity. There may, indeed, be persuasive pastoral reasons for the bishop to be personally present for such occasions. However, there seems to be no canonical reason why the diocesan bishop could not delegate this function to a non-cleric.

Both with regard to chancellors and offices for religious, a certain caution seems in order. Dispensations or faculties which bear directly on the power of orders and its exercise should remain in the hands of clerics, at least until much greater clarity is reached on all that pertains to the power of orders. The changes in the law are new and further examination of their meaning and implications is needed. The exercise of power spoken of in canon 129, §2 is the power of governance. Questions on the interrelatedness of the power of orders and of governance have yet to be addressed.

This interrelatedness is perhaps at the heart of the problem currently being experienced by clerical religious institutes when they wish to ask brother members to serve as superiors. Vatican II provided the impetus for such questions. *Perfectae car-*

itatis urged orders of men to "strengthen the bond of brotherhood" among members, involving brothers more closely in the life and work of the community. Institutes which were not entirely lay were told that they might admit clerics and laymen "on an equal footing and with equal rights and obligations, apart from those arising out of sacred orders" (n. 15). Toward the implementation of this article, *Ecclesiae sanctae* directed general chapters to study how brothers "may, gradually, obtain a vote in specified community activities and in elections, and may even become eligible for certain offices." Their greater involvement in community affairs, the document continued, would allow priests greater freedom for ministries reserved to them (n. 27).

In a further specification of these texts, SCRIS issued the decree *Clericalia instituta* on Nov. 27, 1969. It provided for brothers in clerical institutes to serve in administrative posts and participate fully in chapters. They could serve on councils at all levels. However, "non clerical members will not be able to assume the office of superior or of vicar" (n. 4) at any level. It was expressly stated in this decree that the canons limiting ecclesiastical jurisdiction to clerics was not the root of the problem. In a declaration sent to major superiors the following April, it was further clarified that the fundamental difficulty was "the direction and supervision of priestly ministry" — the administration of sacraments, especially the Eucharist, official preaching, etc. These matters, the declaration stated, require special competence, preparation and the particular ministerial grace of orders. While recognizing the equality of clerical and lay members as religious, and the possibility of brothers possessing even superior giftedness, the brothers were still viewed as lacking the special preparation and "the particular 'social' grace or charism demanded for priestly ministrations."

Much has taken place in the intervening years. The canons now clearly acknowledge that the state of consecrated life, by its very nature, is neither clerical nor lay. Nevertheless, institutes are recognized as being one or the other. An institute is called clerical if, by the intent of its founder or by legitimate tradition it is: a) under the supervision of clerics; b) assumes the exercise of sacred orders; and c) is recognized as clerical by church authority (c. 588).

Among others, Franciscans have resisted this categorization of institutes as inadequate for expressing their reality. At least as early as 1974, an indult was granted as an exception to *Clericalia instituta* 4 allowing a lay brother to serve as local superior "excluding whatever power is connected with the clerical state."

The question was further studied by a 1986 CRIS plenarium. At present, the practice remains that constitutions of clerical institutes cannot be written with general provision for brothers as superiors. However, there is an expressed openness to separate indults which are handled on a case by case basis. Criteria for indults seem to include the qualities and experience of the brother proposed, and the community situation involved, with particular focus on the necessity of the brother superior dealing with pastoral problems of priest members. It is understood that the question will be the object of on-going study.

This was again evident during the 1994 synod on consecrated life, when the status of brothers in clerical institutes was raised in various interventions and in language groups. In his intervention on this subject, Cardinal Rosalio José Castillo Lara noted that the code only defines the two existing categories of institutes, "without precluding — rather insinuating — the possibility of a third." Continuing, however, the cardinal pointed out that the problem remains because superiors of clerical institutes of pontifical right participate in the ecclesiastical power of governance (cf. c. 596, §2) and this does not seem possible to lay superiors. The impossibility arises not only from canon 129 but from the theology enunciated in *Lumen gentium* 18; 21 (19th General Congregation, 14 October 1994).

Even such a cursory review of the question of laity exercising an ecclesiastical power of governance uncovers the issue's complexity. Intensive studies of the teachings of Vatican II and of the nature of the power of orders must continue.

Besides the complexity of the issues, it is likewise evident that the 1983 Code does contain radical changes with regard to the role of lay persons in the life of the Church. The 1981 plenarium's decisive vote to keep the provision for lay participation in the power of governance was crucial. The decision to remove the phrase "not dependent on the power of orders", and the ambiguity which was left regarding the nature of power exercised by lay religious superiors, could be viewed negatively as a pulling back. A more careful consideration of the matter, however, suggests that the drafters of the law deliberately avoided defining matters which needed to remain open.

Sharon Holland, I.H.M.

This article originally appeared in *Bulletin on Issues of Religious Law*, Vol. 4, 1988.

II.
Administrative Issues

7.
VOCATIONAL CRISIS

QUESTION: Can a major superior grant a leave of absence on the basis of canon 665, §1 to a religious experiencing a vocational crisis, who wants to live as a secular lay person in order to decide whether to seek release from religious vows and their obligations, or return to the institute; or should the religious apply for an indult of exclaustration (cc. 686; 687)?

Leave of absence is considered under the chapter dealing with the obligations of religious; one obligation is observance of a common life. Leave of absence addresses a passing situation with a view to resolving a temporary situation regarding study, illness, apostolate, orientation for a new work, etc. When the cause for granting a leave is a vocational crisis, the maximum time which superiors can grant for such leave is one year.

Obviously the member remains such during the period of absence and is held to the observance of the vows, as well as other obligations except those incompatible with the state of absence, such as community exercises. Unless the superior has established other financial arrangements, the authorized indult of absence implicitly gives the member permission to acquire, administer, and use temporal goods in so far as these are necessary for one's appropriate maintenance. The member remains under the authority of superiors and retains active and passive voice.

Exclaustration is similar to leave of absence in some respects, but quite different in others. Exclaustration is presented under the chapter dealing with departure from the institute. Exclaustration requires a "grave" reason, not simply a "just" reason as for a leave (c. 665, §1). Prior consent of the local ordinary where the religious intends to remain is needed in the case of a cleric. Superiors may grant exclaustration for up to three years; extending the indult, or granting it for more than three years, is reserved to the Holy See (or to the bishop for diocesan institutes).

The person who is exclaustrated is free from obligations incompatible with the new condition of life. The person is, however, dependent on and subject to the care of the appropriate religious superiors as well as to the local ordinary, especially if the member is a cleric. The member may wear the habit, unless the indult states the contrary, but lacks both active and passive voice.

Not many would agree with Gallen's assertion that "a vocational decision can almost always be settled in one's own religious house. Untold thousands of men and women decide to marry while living the usual family life." A decision to leave religious life involves radical change in the matter of life style, job training and placement, emotional and personal support systems. Often the person concerned is also confused as to the need for a permanent change, and the ability to cope with all that it involves.

Since superiors are not authorized to extend leave of absence beyond a year, nor to renew the year's permission which had been granted, the maximum time available to experience the secular lifestyle is one year, if a leave is granted.

Institutes have noted that in such situations the first year of the experience outside community is usually spent by the religious in finding a new job and a new living arrangement. Only after this time does the religious have time to consider the vocation problem, which usually takes another two years.

In some cases the superiors grant a member a year's leave to work through some serious emotional problems; during this time, the member realizes that what is at issue is a vocational decision and requests a period of exclaustration to continue to deal with the personal problem. In effect the superiors are able to grant a total of four years, for a serious cause, without having to refer to the Holy See.

It is noted that for cloistered nuns exclaustration is reserved to the Holy See.

To conclude: it would seem preferable to reserve the permission for leaves of absence (up to one year) for cases other than vocational crisis, and to grant an indult of exclaustration for the serious cases of those who are experiencing a vocational crisis, since this normally takes a longer period to resolve. Perhaps, if this becomes a general practice, the term "leave of absence" would lose the connotation of one who is in the process of definitive separation from the community and would regain the sense intended by the code.

Fred Sackett, O.M.I.

This article originally appeared in *Bulletin on Issues of Religious Law*, Vol. 1, 1985.

8.
INDEFINITE LEAVE OF ABSENCE

Religious have an obligation to live in a house of their institute. To live elsewhere, even in the house of another religious community, requires permission of the superior who is competent according to the constitutions to grant such permission. In three instances — care of poor health, studies, or the undertaking of an apostolate in the name of the institute — a major superior with the consent of his/her council is authorized to permit a member to reside outside a house of the institute for as long as the case requires (c. 665, §1). In other kinds of cases, where there is a just reason, a major superior with the consent of his/her council may permit a prolonged absence, but not for more than a year.

>   1. When illness or poor health is the cause for the leave of absence, any kind of illness suffices, whether physical or mental, as long as there is question of a true illness either in the technical sense or in the ordinary meaning of the term. Any stage of illness or poor health, and any degree of intensity qualifies. Since the canon no longer requires a serious cause but only a just cause, even a slight illness is cause enough, if the other conditions are verified. One who is convalescing from a sickness is still in poor health, and for that reason leave of absence could begin or be extended during that period, even though the sickness was over.
>
>   The superior and council should consider whether poor health or sickness is present; whether leave will be helpful, as well as the time, place and other circumstances of the leave. In some cases transfer to another house of the institute might provide a needed change of climate when that is the cause of poor health.
>
>   In determining whether illness is present and whether a leave will be beneficial, the doctor's advice and the views of the person concerned are given great weight. Sometimes that person is the only one who can really determine the state of health, and whether or not a leave would be helpful. A prudent decision often depends on the psychological state of the patient and on the nature and effects of the illness. Note that the illness meant in the canon is one which afflicts the religious member, not a relative of the member.
>
>   2. A leave granted for the purpose of studies is justified whether one is taking a course of studies, for example a student or a researcher, or whether one is teaching a course of studies. Some commentators, however, consider teaching to constitute a valid reason for indefinite leave only when it is "an apostolate in the name of the institute."
>
>   3. Apostolate undertaken in the name of the institute. Apostolate here should be interpreted in the broad sense; it includes not only work which is specifically pastoral, such as care of a parish, chaplaincy of another religious

community, catechizing, but also other kinds of teaching, public health nursing, social work and the like, provided that the work engaged in is in conformity with the purpose of the religious institute. Commentators interpret this provision broadly, so that in practice only apostolic works forbidden to members in a given institute cannot be considered as connected with its purpose; all other kinds of apostolate, whether proper to the institute, or simply permitted or tolerated are connected with its purpose.

4. Leave granted for other just reasons is not to exceed one year. If, however, the religious returns to a house of the community for a period of time sufficient to break its legal continuity, and if the just reason persists, the religious could request and the competent superior (with the consent of the council) could permit the same religious to take another leave of absence, for up to a year. To illustrate: If the member returned to a house of the community for the Christmas or Easter season or at any other time simply for a break from the work outside, or to renew comradeship with the other religious, or to make one's annual retreat, and if this sojourn with the community lasted a week or more, there would be a sufficient break in the flow of time to effect an interruption of the previous grant of absence and thus pave the way for another grant if it were judged to be justified on the basis of a just cause.

A religious on leave of absence is still a full-fledged member of the community. General permissions in many financial matters will have to be granted. As for obedience, the member remains bound to superiors and must submit reports as required. The member also has a right to all notices from superiors and retains active and passive voice.

5. As is well known, there are special provisions in the law for cloistered nuns. Canon 667, §4 states that "for a grave cause and with the consent of the superior, (the diocesan bishop can permit) nuns to leave the cloister for a truly necessary period of time." The Instruction *Venite seorsum* (Aug. 15, 1969) authorized the superior with at least the habitual consent of the diocesan bishop to permit a short leave from the cloister for a just cause, for example to consult the doctor, to exercise civil rights; if the absence must be protracted beyond a week the consent of the diocesan bishop and of the regular superior, if there is one, is needed; permission of the Holy See is needed for absence over three months. It is safe to assume that these guidelines may still be followed. It is not too clear that the Holy See must be approached for an absence over three months; the revised code seems to leave the matter to the diocesan bishop.

Fred Sackett, O.M.I.

This article originally appeared in *Bulletin on Issues of Religious Law*, Vol. 1, 1985.

9.
COMPLEMENTARY COMPETENCIES: BISHOPS, SUPERIORS, AND APOSTOLATES

Vatican II addressed the relationship between religious and bishops with respect to apostolic works or ministries in *Christus Dominus* (*CD*), the Decree on the Pastoral Office of Bishops.

Various forms of apostolates should be encouraged and ... the coordination and close interrelationship of all apostolic works in the entire diocese should be promoted under the direction of the bishop. In this way all enterprises and organizations ... should be brought into harmonious activity (*CD* 17).

With this statement a fundamental principle is clearly established, that the bishop is to oversee, coordinate and moderate all apostolic activity in his diocese. This conciliar position was then cast in juridical language in canon 394, §1 of the revised code:

> The bishop should encourage various kinds of apostolate in his diocese and should take care that all works of the apostolate in the entire diocese are coordinated under his direction, safeguarding the proper character of each.

When addressing the relationship between religious and the diocesan bishop the same decree of the Council stated that "all religious ... are subject to the power of local ordinaries in what pertains to ... various works which concern the exercise of the sacred apostolate" (*CD* 35, 4). This, too, is restated in canonical language in canon 678, §1: "Religious are subject to the power of the bishop ... in those matters which ... concern works of the apostolate.

It is obvious that the bishop will have to rely heavily upon the assistance of religious men and women to accomplish successfully his own office of teaching, sanctifying and governing in the particular church, and it is equally clear that religious can provide such assistance only within the scope of "the nature, purpose, spirit and character" of their respective institutes (c. 578). Indeed, religious were seen by the Council as very important helpers of the bishops in the apostolic efforts of the dioceses. Religious priests belong "in a certain genuine sense ... to the clergy of the diocese inasmuch as they share ... in carrying out works of the apostolate under the authority of the sacred prelates." Likewise, religious who are not priests "also belong in a special way to the diocesan family. They provide great assistance to the sacred hierarchy and should provide it in an ever-increasing degree" (*CD* 34). It is clear, therefore, that Vatican II did not recognize any undertaking as apostolic which eluded the authority of the bishop to oversee it, to integrate it into the diocesan pastoral ministry, and to provide overall direction to it.

The Council, however, singled out one form of apostolate, Catholic schools, for special attention and in doing so introduced a distinction between "the schools of religious" and, by implication, other Catholic schools. It stated that the schools of religious are subject to the general policy established for Catholic schools by the bishop and to his oversight, "but the right of the religious to direct them remains intact" (*CD* 34). *Ecclesiae sanctae* 1, 39 (1) identified general policy as dealing with the distribution of Catholic schools, their mutual cooperation, and the bishop's oversight aimed at the development of excellence in Catholic education.

The code, too, gives special attention to schools in canon 806, §1, which speaks of the role of oversight and the right of visitation by the bishop and of his right to establish diocesan policies for all Catholic schools, while safe-guarding the autonomy of religious regarding the internal governance of their own schools. Apart from schools, however, neither the Council nor the code qualifies the role of the bishop with respect to all apostolic and ministerial undertakings in his diocese.

I. Corporate Apostolates and Contracts

Religious participate in the apostolate of a diocese either corporately or individually. Corporate apostolate here means that the religious institute as such undertakes to provide, on at least a relatively permanent basis, a specific service in the pastoral mission of a diocese. They do this in two ways, by accepting an invitation either to establish a specific apostolic enterprise of their own, for example, a school, hospital, residence for the aged; or to provide staffing for a diocesan work, for example, a parish, a diocesan high school, a retreat center.

In either case a contract should be entered into and the parties to the contract are the two juridic persons, the diocese and the religious institute, acting through their canonical representatives, the bishop or his delegate and the appropriate religious superior. In the case of a diocesan work confided to a religious community, the code requires a formal contract in canon 681, §2; in the case of religious establishing a work of their own, the written consent of the bishop, required by canon 609, §1, constitutes the formal agreement between the parties (cf. c. 611, 2°). These documents should carefully spell out the respective competencies of the bishop or other diocesan official and of the religious superiors.

The bishop, however, cannot bargain away the responsibility that is his to oversee and coordinate all apostolic undertakings in his diocese (c. 394, §1). The religious superior, on the other hand, cannot commit the institute in a manner which is disallowed by its own law or policies. The parties must arrive at mutual agreement before signing a covenant with each other. This is the meaning of *collatis consiliis* in canon 678, §3, a significantly stronger expression than "mutual consultation."

What should such contracts or covenants include? The code itself indicates in a general way that, in the case of diocesan work to be confided to religious, the written agreement should include, among other things, whatever pertains to the work itself, which implies that it is clearly defined; the members to be engaged in it and financial matters (c. 681, §2). The phrase, "among other things," suggests that the parties to the contract should agree upon any other stipulations which either or both sides deem necessary or appropriate. Such matters could be the duration and the periodic review of the agreement itself, the mission and goals of the enterprise, the lines and the scope of authority and accountability, procedures for the appointment and termination of personnel and their qualifications, and similar issues.

In a work proper to the religious institute, such stipulations should be spelled out in whatever detail seems appropriate to either party in the proposal made by the institute and agreed to by the bishop, that is, in the written consent of canons 609, §1 and 611, 2°. If these agreements are properly developed, the reciprocal rights and duties of the diocesan bishop and the religious superiors will be clearly understood, and disagreements and friction should thereby be minimized.

II. Diocesan Apostolates of Individuals

Religious also participate in the pastoral ministry of a diocese as individuals. They are frequently appointed to diocesan offices as superintendents of schools, pastors, associate pastors, episcopal vicars, directors of various offices, chancellors, and other like responsibilities. The religious superior who agrees to such an appointment and thereby missions the member to this apostolic work or ministry has little, if any, authority with respect to the work to be accomplished or the service to be rendered, since this is determined by the universal or particular law, or by the bishop or his delegates, and depends entirely upon the bishop. The superior, however, is not relieved of the responsibility which the proper law of the institute defines. He or she is called upon to promote and safeguard the religious life of the member, and the individual religious remains bound by the commitment made in religious profession. The superior should also provide appropriate assistance in fulfilling the member's office as effectively as possible.

The code does not mention a contract or written agreement between the diocese or a diocesan entity (except for a parish — cf. c. 520, §2) and the individual religious or the institute itself in such cases. Such employment contracts, nevertheless, are common today and, given the nature of religious life, necessarily make the institute itself a party to the arrangement. Quite often the contract is signed both by the individual religious and the appropriate superior, acting on behalf of the institute or province. These contracts, however, can be canonically problematic. The reason for this is canon 682, §2, which establishes the right of the bishop and of the religious superior to remove a religious from an office, even if the term of the appointment has not expired, provided that prior notice has been given the bishop or the superior.

Can this right be waived by the bishop and the superior? Certainly anyone can commit himself or herself not to exercise a right except in unusual circumstances and for the procedures to be followed if they arise, including the time of notification to the bishop or the superior. Without such a contractual arrangement this canon is operative.

III. Private Apostolates

For want of a better expression, what is meant here by a private apostolate, which is an apparent contradiction in terms, is an enterprise or work undertaken by an individual religious with at least the tacit approval of superiors. This activity is such that it eludes integration into the pastoral goals and planning of a diocese and is usually considered secular. Examples of this kind of undertaking would be teaching in a public school, practicing law or medicine, accounting or nursing apart from a church-related institution, working as a probation officer or as a county social worker. Employment of this kind cannot be termed apostolic or a ministry in the sense of the Council or the code.

In the case of a religious priest, the bishop has the right to judge the occupation as improper and to require that it be terminated. In the case of a lay religious, the bishop can more easily approve of it. In either case the work is considered more appropriate to lay persons who are not religious and especially for members of secular institutes. The final judgment about this, however, rests with the bishop in consultation with the religious superior.

IV. Conclusion

It is evident that the code does not spell out in detail the respective competencies or jurisdictions of the diocesan bishop and religious superiors whose companions are engaged in ministries or apostolates in a diocese. It rests satisfied with a more general norm by articulating their respective roles, thus leaving to particular law and to decisions mutually arrived at, the precise determination of the authority of the bishop and the institute with respect to such works. In doing this there is a clear need for written agreements so that the diocese and the institute can work together in harmony for the welfare of the People of God.

Richard A. Hill, S.J.

This article originally appeared in *Bulletin on Issues of Religious Law*, Vol. 1, 1985.

10.
DISPENSATION AND DISMISSAL

The terms dispensation and dismissal are commonly used to refer to the manner in which a religious becomes definitively separated from his or her institute and ceases to be a religious either through a process initiated by one's self or through a process initiated by one's competent superior. Technically, in the new code, the phrase "indult of departure" refers to the result of this process when it has been initiated by the member. It is used in this manner in canons 688, §2; 691, §§1 and 2; 692; and 693. The phrase "indult of secularization" used in canon 684, §2 was probably retained due to an editing oversight (since this was the term used in the former code and it appears nowhere else in the new one), and it really means "indult of departure" as just described. Technically, the word dispensation refers to the legal effect either of an "indult of departure" or of "dismissal," that is, the cessation of one's vows and the rights and obligations resulting from profession. In canon 692 this legal effect is a favor; in canon 701, it is a deprivation.

There are other forms of separation from one's religious institute which do not qualify either as an "indult of departure" or as "dismissal." One is transfer (cc. 684-685), the process by which a religious alters his or her institute of membership while remaining a religious. Another is exclaustration (cc. 686-687), the vehicle through which a religious remains a member of one's institute but has mitigated rights and obligations with respect to common life and some vows. Still another is departure from the institute at the expiration of one's time of temporary profession (c. 688, §1). There is the mistaken notion among many religious that legitimate permission to be absent from the house according to canon 665, §1 is also some form of departure from an institute. This is simply incorrect since such absence does not alter a member's status in the institute whatsoever. It is a legal provision for exceptions to the obligation of common life, and the provision is not even included in the canons on separation (cc. 684-704).

Although the canons of the code are not organized in this manner, it is helpful to deal with the topic of separation by dividing it into "voluntary" (self-initiated) and "involuntary" (other-initiated) categories. When this is done, the canonical means of separation from an institute can be conveniently summarized as follows:

A. VOLUNTARY SEPARATION

(1) Permission to Transfer — canons 684 and 685

(2) Indult of Exclaustration — canons 686 and 687

(3) Expiration of Vows — canon 688, §1

(4) Indult of Departure for Temporary Vows — canon 688, §2

(5) Indult of Departure for Perpetual Vows — canon 691

B. Involuntary Separation

(1) Categorical Refusal of Consideration for Transfer — canon 684, §§1 and 3

(2) Imposed Exclaustration — canon 686, §3

(3) Exclusion from Renewal/Final Profession — canon 689, §§1 and 2

(4) Automatic Dismissal — canon 694, §§1 and 2

(5) Mandatory Dismissal — canon 695, §§1 and 2

(6) Discretionary Dismissal — canon 696, §1

A. Voluntary Separation

Within the "voluntary" category of separation, category (3) is the most simple type both from the perspective of procedures and consequences: whenever the time of temporary vows has elapsed the member is free from his or her vows as well as from all rights and obligations that arose from profession (c. 688, §1). Within the same category and posing minimal problems procedurally is A(4): the member requests to depart, and the indult of departure can be granted by the supreme moderator of a pontifical institute with consent of council. For diocesan institutes or for monasteries that have no competent authority between them and the Apostolic See, the indult granted by the supreme moderator with consent of council is invalid unless confirmed by the bishop of the place in which the house to which the member is assigned is located. For A(5) the procedure is the same, but the supreme moderator does not grant the indult. He or she transmits the petition, along with his or her opinion and that of the council, either to the Apostolic See or to the bishop (as mentioned above) and these can grant the indult of departure. One difference in the present law from the recent practice of CICLSAL is that the indult takes effect upon notification unless rejected (c. 692). In A(3) departure is a right. In A(4) and (5) it is not a right but a favor that may or may not be granted by the competent authority subsequent to the member's petition. In all three the legal result is the same: the member no longer belongs to any religious institute.

Consent to transfer to another institute, A(1), is not a right for religious, and it may or may not be granted depending on the judgment of competent authorities mentioned in canon 684, §§1 and 3. Several items are important regarding transfers. First, these canons obtain only for transfers to or from religious institutes and do not apply to transfers to or from secular institutes or societies of apostolic life or the categories of hermits (c. 603) or consecrated virgins (c. 604). These alterations of status must be processed through the Apostolic See (§5). Second, the time of probation for transfer (§2) does not require making a novitiate, but the duration of probation must be for a period of no less than three years. Third, the time of probation begins to be counted only after all required permissions are obtained. Fourth, the member in process of transfer under §1 retains legal membership in the originating institute with the right and obligation of returning to it should he or she not be accepted for profession in the new institute.

An indult of exclaustration, A(2), is not a right for the member of any institute but depends on the judgment of the supreme moderator who requires consent of council in order to grant it validly. It can be granted only to those who are perpetually professed and only for a period of up to three years. Because of the ambiguous wording of the Latin text of the two sentences in canon 686, §1, there is some debate among canonists as to whether going beyond the initial grant (if initially made for only one or two years) or whether going beyond the three year limit is the determining factor for having recourse to the Apostolic See or to the diocesan bishop. Some say that after the initial indult of exclaustration is granted, even if it extends for less than three years, the higher authority must be approached if the member wishes to continue on exclaustration. Others say that a three year limit (by any combination of years) has been the recent consistent practice of the Apostolic See for such indults and that the second sentence of the paragraph is included to prevent the issuance of repeated indults of three years. Linguistic analysis of the Latin does not shed light on the debate; the discussions of the study group that formulated this canon are not yet available; and an authentic interpretation of the text has not been made by Rome. Thus, either interpretation is legitimate (provided one does not go beyond three years in all), and the one that is most advantageous may be followed in a particular case.

In A(1), (2) and (5) above, members of clerical institutes have additional requirements to be aware of in relation to incardination (cc. 266 and 693) and the exercise of orders (c. 687); and the process is further complicated if the cleric wishes also to be laicized (cc. 290-292).

B. Involuntary Separation

Categorical refusal of consideration for transfer, B(1), is listed under involuntary separation because an across-the-board policy of non-consideration of requests for transfer in fact requires any member to seek an indult of departure so that he or she may enter another institute. The universal law provides a vehicle for transfer so that a religious may alter the legal connection to this or that institute without departing from religious life as such. In some sense categorical non-consideration constitutes a restriction, if not a violation, of the acquired right of members (c. 654) to continue to live religious life. Any restriction of acquired rights is to be interpreted strictly (c. 18), that is, in a way allowing the greatest possible exercise of the right. Note, however, that any religious does not have a right to be granted permission to transfer, but rather has the right after perpetual profession to continue living religious life and, therefore, should not be denied this right by a policy of non-consideration of possible transfer procedures.

A request for imposed exclaustration, B(2), is made by the supreme moderator with the consent of council. Those competent to impose exclaustration are the

Apostolic See for pontifical institutes and the diocesan bishop for diocesan institutes. The procedure to be followed is known from practice to be the same as that for dismissal [see below, B(6)] but applied in a somewhat less rigorous manner. The primary difference between voluntary and imposed exclaustration is that a religious under imposed exclaustration may not return to live in the institute without the intervention of the competent authority who imposed the exclaustration. Any exclaustrated religious: (1) may wear the habit of the institute (unless the indult indicates otherwise); (2) is still bound by vow but is excused from those rights and obligations of profession (such as common life and financial arrangements) that are less than compatible with the circumstances of exclaustration; (3) is still subject to the institute's superiors as well as dependent on the local ordinary; and (4) may neither vote nor receive votes in any election of the institute. Mutual rights, obligations and expectations for the period of exclaustration should be very clear to both the exclaustrated member and the institute, and these should be in writing.

Exclusion from renewal of profession or from perpetual profession by canon 689, §§1 or 2, although a form of involuntary departure, is not as such a violation of the right to live religious life. This is because the rights of membership affirmed in canon 654 are legally qualified for those in temporary vows by the subsequent decisions of the major superior acting with the advice of council (c. 689, §1). Such exclusion does, however, require just causes (plural); and these causes should relate directly to the substantive content of the institute's formation program or the proper charism of the institute or to the requirements of consecrated life itself. One just cause for non-admission that is given specific legal mention in §2 is a physical or psychic infirmity that renders the religious inept for leading the life of the institute. Note, however, that the judgment of experts (i.e., qualified professional persons) is required, that the infirmity cannot have been acquired due to work in or negligence of the institute, and that the burden of proof in this regard is on the institute (not on the excluded member). Charity and justice certainly dictate that any exclusion ought not to be a surprise to the member concerned and that the reasons for exclusion ought to be communicated to the person at least in summary form and in the best possible manner for the good of all concerned.

There are three sub-categories of "dismissal" that result in definitive separation from one's institute. These are: automatic; mandatory; and discretionary dismissal, corresponding to B(4), (5) and (6) above. It is important to note that all situations warranting dismissal must be treated in the same manner as are penalties (cc. 1311-1399). That is, the law regarding them must be strictly interpreted using the exact canonical meaning of the words (c. 18), and none of the required procedures may be omitted or dispensed (c. 87). It is also important to note that no one is subject to a penalty unless there are objective, subjective, and juridic elements present. There must be an external violation of a law or precept which (violation) is gravely imputable to the person either from malice or culpability and there is some juridic attention to the offense (c. 1321). Furthermore, the law itself lists many excusing and mitigating circumstances (cc. 1323 and 1324) in which no one is liable to a penalty as indicated. Finally, in the canons on dismissal from religious life, there is no instance in which the competent authorities [i.e., major superior (cc. 694, §2; 695,

§1; 697) and supreme moderator (cc. 698; 699, §1)] can act validly without at least the advice of council, and it should be obvious that they should never attempt to act in a situation that appears to warrant dismissal without the advice of experienced canonists.

Automatic dismissal (c. 694) is distinctly different from the other two types because in such cases the action of the member, rather than the action of the major superior, is what actually renders the religious dismissed. The action of the major superior is important, however, to declare and thus establish as juridic fact that the automatic dismissal has been incurred. This is important because both offenses listed in canon 694, §1 which result in automatic dismissal, i.e., notorious defection from the faith (n. 1) and attempted marriage (n. 2), are also treated in Book VI of the code, "On Sanctions," in canons 1364, §1 and 1394, §2. If such sanctions are not properly "declared" according to law, then the observance of their consequences is suspended in certain circumstances (c. 1335).

For the mandatory dismissal of canon 695, §1, the canons, rather than the actual offenses as in canon 694, §1, are listed in the code. Although it says that members must be dismissed for the offenses included here [i.e., homicide, abduction, detention, mutilation, infliction of grave wounds (c. 1397), procuring an abortion (c. 1398), and clerical concubinage or sins against the sixth commandment (c. 1395)], it is quite clear in penal law that the competent superior (c. 1342, §3) is granted wide discretion in whether or not to defer application of the penalty (c. 1344, 1° and 2°), even if the words of the law are preceptive. In cases of mandatory dismissal, after the requirements of canon 695 have been followed, the procedures of canons 698; 699 and 700 still apply.

The wording of canon 695, §1 makes it obvious that initiation of the dismissal process for the offenses listed therein is discretionary. Without looking at the process in detail, note that the following elements are indispensable:

(1) a serious, external, imputable, proven action on the part of the accused;

(2) a decision, after consultation, to initiate the process;

(3) collection of proof for the elements of n. 1;

(4) two clear indications to the accused, with intervening time for amendment, of both the offense and possible dismissal; and

(5) ability of the accused to present a defense, including the right to communicate directly with the supreme moderator (c. 698).

If a decision is finally made to issue a decree of dismissal, the rules for decrees obtain (cc. 48-58); and whether it is issued by the supreme moderator acting collegially with council (for pontifical and diocesan institutes) or by the diocesan bishop (for monasteries that qualify under c. 615), it must contain summary reasons in fact and in law for the actions taken (cc. 699 and 51). Any decree so issued must also be confirmed by a higher authority (CICLSAL or the diocesan bishop) and is invalid if it does not indicate the right of suspensive recourse within ten days of notification (c. 700).

It might be noted that, for the most part, it is extremely difficult to dismiss a perpetually professed member from a religious institute. In fact, this area of the law and the manner in which it is consistently applied is highly protective of the right of a duly professed member to continue in the institute even for those situations in which his or her behavior may be obviously less than what is expected or adequate. Moreover, experience indicates that many persons in positions of authority who have responsibility to initiate these procedures are extremely cautious, if not reluctant, to act unless almost forced to do so. Consequently, two problematic situations are not uncommon. On the one hand, repeatedly disruptive and less than acceptable behavior on the part of some religious is tolerated sometimes to the extreme individual and collective detriment of others in the community. On the other hand, extremely peripheral and minimal (if any) manifestation of membership is allowed on the part of those who are not troublesome although they appear at times to be no more than juridically members of the institute.

Indeed, at the heart of both these problematic situations — and central to the entire discussion of any of the categories mentioned above — is not so much the question of separation as that of what constitutes membership in any religious institute. Persons in positions of religious governance often "inherit" long-term (and at times poorly dealt-with) problems from previous administrations and find it difficult to "move in" on these situations without appearing authoritarian and legalistic. Yet continued non-attention to regularly troublesome or admittedly marginal members is, in the long run, quite counter-productive because of its inevitable toll in overall energy consumption and its eventual detrimental effect on individual and collective morale. In fact, if the meaning of membership is addressed as the central issue in the various categories of voluntary separation and involuntary separation, the applicability of each category is much clearer and the dialogical relationship of responsibility and concern between the member and those in positions of authority is much more meaningful. This emphasis also places the decisions of members in regard to transfer or exclaustration or departure and the actions of superiors in regard to imposed exclaustration or non-acceptance or dismissal squarely in the context of the rights and obligations freely assumed at profession. These rights and obligations are knowingly and freely assumed in the first person singular, but they are lived out in the context of community in relation to others according to constitutional norms that, at the very best, express only minimally what it means to "belong" to any religious institute. Universal law recognizes that, humanly speaking, one's status of "belonging" may require legal alteration and, thus, provides for various modalities of "separation."

Elizabeth McDonough, O.P.

This article originally appeared in *Bulletin on Issues of Religious Law*, Vol. 2, 1986.

11.
Selecting a Canonical Advisor

How do you select a canon lawyer? Very carefully! There is more to this old saying than humor, for there are several reasons to select a canonical advisor with great care.

The first is that not all canon lawyers are trained in the law as it relates to religious institutes. Canon law covers a variety of concerns, from the structures and operations of parishes, dioceses, and the Church universal, to questions about sacraments, seminary education, the life and work of church ministers, etc. The canons on institutes of consecrated life form a special area within the overall law of the Church, and many canon lawyers have not had the training or inclination to become expert in this area. So, just because a person has a canon law degree does not mean that person would necessarily be a knowledgeable advisor in the canon law on religious.

Another factor is that not everyone who is in a position one might normally consider the domain of a canon lawyer has professional canon law training. Increasingly there are fewer people staffing diocesan chanceries with degrees in canon law. Even the staff persons of diocesan tribunals, who theoretically are required to have degrees in canon law, may include a number of people who began to work there before this requirement took effect and do not have degrees. So, the fact that a person holds a position which traditionally was held by a degreed canon lawyer does not necessarily mean that person is a canon lawyer.

A third factor is that canon lawyers, like everyone else in the Church, have differing sensitivities to the meaning of the Church and to the role of religious life in the Church. These personal perspectives can influence how a particular canonist approaches the job and may produce differing views on the application of church law to specific cases. Just as a person would carefully evaluate the approach a doctor, dentist, or civil lawyer takes, so the approach of individual canon lawyers needs to be taken into consideration in selecting a canonical advisor. Not all canonists are the same; it is important to pay attention to the differences.

A fourth element to keep in mind is that the interpretation of canon law admits of various opinions. Unless there has been an authoritative interpretation from the Pontifical Council for the Interpretation of Legislative Texts, the various opinions carry the weight of the reasons which support them. It is not a question of the number of people who hold a particular opinion, but rather of the relative merits of the reasons which support that opinion. Thus, if several canon lawyers are asked about a particular point, and various opinions are expressed, it may easily be that any one of those opinions may be followed provided it has serious reasons to support it and does not violate the rights of anyone. What is important here is for the person who is seeking the canonical advice to have a good understanding of this point from the beginning.

Approaching the quest for canonical advisor, therefore, requires the same good sense as approaching the search for any advisor. Keeping these cautions in mind, how can canon lawyers be located? There are several possibilities.

As with other advisors, word of mouth and recommendations from others with experience can help identify trustworthy canonical advisors. Canonists who write on topics in religious law often can be contacted through the journals for which they write. Some have found it useful to contact the Executive Coordinator of the Canon Law Society of America. The Coordinator's office does not maintain a list of religious canonists, but is able to discuss an individual's needs and eventually suggest several members of the Society who might be able to help.

When selecting canonical advisors, it may be helpful to consult two or three at the beginning. See who is able to relate more effectively to the situation at hand, whose advice is more understandable, which opinions seem to be more carefully supported with sound reasons. It is not necessary, or even appropriate in some circumstances, to continue to consult a number of canonists once a reliable canonical advisor has been located. However, one should beware of the single expert; it may prove helpful from time to time to check with others. This can maintain confidence in the advisor of choice but may also serve to maintain a proper perspective on the diversity which is appropriate in canonical interpretation.

How much does canonical advice cost? Normally, advisors must have their expenses reimbursed, particularly if travel is involved. Many canon lawyers work full-time for the Church and donate their services. Some rely on fees from consultations and lectures for a major portion of their income. In October, 1995 the Canon Law Society of America adopted "Guidelines on Advocates' Reimbursement and Fees," which state that if an advocate charges fees, they may be "on a daily or hourly basis, or as a flat fee for specific services. Depending on the nature of the case, economic circumstances, and the expertise required, a fee within the range of $50 to $100 per hour is reasonable. A canonist can charge a lower fee for persons of meager income." Do not hesitate to ask a canonist what stipend may be expected.

There are many women and men canon lawyers who are dedicated to serving the Church and who are interested in providing you with competent canonical advice. A certain amount of ordinary caution will provide both you and them with a satisfactory relationship.

James H. Provost

This article originally appeared in *Bulletin on Issues of Religious Law*, Vol. 2, 1986.

12.
THE MERGER AND UNION OF RELIGIOUS INSTITUTES

I. WHY CONSIDER MERGER OR UNION?

Before the recent decrease in the number of religious, the Holy See was already concerned with institutes that did not "offer any reasonable hope for further development" (*Perfectae caritatis* 21). In such cases the institute was not to receive any more novices and, if possible, to be united to a more flourishing institute whose aim and spirit was similar to its own (*Ecclesiae sanctae* 39-41).

Following the Decree on the Renewal of Religious Life, the available statistics show that most of the decrees for merger or union were issued in the late 1960s through the early 1970s. They were primarily for European institutes. Since 1980 there have been few mergers or unions reported. However, it may be that the time has come for other institutes to consider merger or union.

The reasons that may prompt an institute to consider union or merger are usually one or several of the following:

> 1. The absence of any new members or few new members over an extended period of time.
>
> 2. The number of members has been significantly decreased through death and departure.
>
> 3. The members of the institute have serious difficulty in caring for their ministries or their members.
>
> 4. Difficulty in obtaining financial support for care of members and ministries.

Since these causes are usually related, many institutes experience all or most of them as a prelude to merger or union. It should be noted that although the above reasons all relate to survival of the institute, there is no reason why two or more strong and healthy institutes cannot merge or unite to provide more efficient administration and enhance or extend their service in ministry. In fact, institutes may prevent or minimize factors that adversely affect survival by anticipating them and by merging or uniting to support the continued life of the institutes. The text of the law does not limit mergers or unions to particular reasons. At the same time, it should be understood that merger or union may not resolve certain difficulties facing religious institutes so that going out of existence may be the appropriate solution in some cases.

II. Defining Merger and Union

At this time the practice of the Holy See and the usage of canonists is in the process of clarifying the meaning of the terms merger and union as used in canon 582 which states:

> Mergers and unions of consecrated life are reserved to the Apostolic See alone; confederations and federations are also reserved to it.

For the purposes of this paper, merger refers to one institute joining another so that the joining institute loses its own juridic identity as an institute and agrees to accept the juridic identity of the institute which it joins. Although the joining institute may lose its juridic identity as an institute, it may receive some identifiable juridic identity within the receiving institute such as a province or a region.

In a union, the joining institutes lose their former juridic identity and receive a new juridic identity. Even in a union the institutes may agree to retain the name and/or constitutions of one of the institutes for practical reasons. As in a merger, the institutes may retain some juridic status as a province or a region.

The requirement of canon 582 is that petitions for merger or union are reserved to the Holy See. This is true even if both institutes are diocesan institutes.

III. Factors to Consider

Although the number of factors that will lead to the decision to seek merger or union will be influenced by the situation, some of the common factors are:

1. Charism. Is there enough of a similarity in the "nature, purpose, spirit and character" (c. 578) and its "wholesome traditions" (c. 578) to believe that the institutes can adjust to life together? For instance, it would be difficult for a contemplative institute to join an apostolic institute and form a cohesive unit. Charism, in fact, touches most of the remaining factors.

2. Lifestyle. Has the institute lived in small or large communities or both? What are the personnel policies? Are assignments usually initiated by the community or the individual or are both allowable? What is the understanding and norms regarding the vow of poverty? Is the custom to have individual budgets or allowances?

3. Ministries. Are the ministries more institutional or non-institutional? Is there a tradition of being educated for the ministries of health care, education, etc.? Is ministry focused on a particular group such as the poor, uneducated, unchurched, rural or racial or ethnic background?

4. Culture. Many institutes originated in a particular culture or country. If the customs of the institute are rooted in a particular culture, it may make amalgamation with another institute difficult.

5. Geography. Institutes that have worked primarily in a certain region such as the Northeast and Midwest, etc., may find the fusion difficult if it is expected that members will be transferred to another region of the country.

6. Spirituality. Institutes which have a common spiritual tradition such as Benedictine, Carmelite, Ignatian, or Franciscan have a natural spiritual background to rely on when they join. Institutes from different traditions may experience difficulty because of previous training and lived experience.

7. Government. This refers to both the structure of the constitutions and the manner in which leadership is exercised. Institutes with highly centralized government, wide ranging authority in superiors and directive processes may find it difficult to join institutes which are more decentralized, consultive and participative in orientation.

8. Size. Relative size may be important since a large institute may tend to dominate in a merger or union. This can provide a feeling of a lack of participation or voice or loss of identity.

9. Psychological Effects. These are both personal and corporate. Identity on both levels is important. Matters such as the name of the institute, identifying signs, the history and tradition (written and oral) will be areas in which great sensitivity must be exercised. For individuals, personal trauma such as experiencing the death of a part of self, facing an unknown future, being accountable to new leadership or need to change a way of life may confront them.

10. Civil Law Organization. In each case, study of the present civil law structure of both the institutes and their apostolates will be necessary in order to develop the best civil law structure to serve the new merger or union. This includes matters such as insurance and pensions or retirement benefits.

11. Finances. Will the combined finances present a stronger financial situation or will the merged or united institutes be weaker? Sometimes, even a financially healthy institute may not be able to undertake the financial debts and burdens of another institute.

IV. THE PROCESS

The process is well defined in a response from the Congregation for Religious to two institutes that received a decree of union:

1. The Sacred Congregation requires first of all that there be a suitable preparation by the Sisters whose lives will be affected by this decision.

2. It is recommended that you be helped by an expert or canonist who can

explain to the Sisters what is involved in the proposed union and answer their questions.

3. There must be study, prayer, and discernment on the part of the Sisters.

4. Some helpful means in preparing the Sisters spiritually, and also psychologically, for the union are opportunities for common week-ends of prayer, inter-community retreats, preliminary acquaintance with the approved constitutions of the large institute, informal gatherings through which the Sisters get to know one another.

5. Of primary importance is that each Sister of the amalgamating institute be entirely free in making her choice to be part of the union or to transfer to another religious institute, or to request a dispensation from her vows.

6. Juridically, the Congregation for Religious requires the secret formal vote of the Sisters of the amalgamating institute in the greatest possible majority. Secondly, the written opinion and approval of the Diocesan Bishop, and a preliminary fundamental agreement for the disposition of temporalities according to the norms of law.

7. The Sacred Congregation also requires the declaration of acceptance of the receiving institute. If the latter institute is not large, the declaration may come from the General Chapter, if opportune, or from a Special Assembly. If the receiving institute is large, it is sufficient that the declaration of acceptance be given by the General Superior and her Council and by the Provincial Superiors and their Councils or by the enlarged General Council of the Institute.

8. In addition to these documents listed above, it is desirable that this office receive a list of the Sisters of the amalgamating institute with their dates of birth and profession, a brief history of the process toward union, and the reasons for the request.

Numbers 1, 2, 3 and 4 are important matters because they center on the preparation of members by a consideration of each important factor in a merger or union, so that as complete an understanding and knowledge of the process and its result as possible is conveyed to everyone concerned. This is perhaps the most important part of the process. Even if all the canonical and legal areas are in order, if this preparation does not result in sufficient understanding and knowledge, the proposed merger or union will be extremely difficult.

Numbers 5, 6, 7 and 8 focus on legal and administrative matters which require specific documentation in support of the petition. It is clear that a member must be free to accept the decision of institutes to merge or unite. This may present a difficult choice for the member who prefers matters as they are. The member may not like any of the options: to be part of the merged or united institute, to transfer, or to request a dispensation from vows. The difficulty that some members may face in regard to the options is why the Congregation looks for the "greatest possible majority" in a vote by the members of the institute. The Congregation does not want to create more problems than a merger or union would solve.

The Congregation also gives great respect to the opinion and approval of the diocesan bishops(s). This refers to the diocesan bishop of a diocesan institute and usually the diocesan bishop in whose diocese a pontifical institute has its principle office.

The first step in the process occurs within the institute seeking merger or union. It involves a study of all the factors listed above with regard to themselves and, to the extent possible, of the potential institutes for merger or union. The second step occurs within the potential institutes for union or merger. If they make the preliminary decision to consider merger or union they undergo a similar study of the same factors.

If after the preliminary consideration by the institutes it is decided to proceed further, the next step is to engage in a series of procedures that allows the members of the institutes to get to know and understand each other on a person-to-person basis. Some of the processes used by institutes include exchange of newsletters, reports (on ministry and finances), joint meetings of leadership (councils and parallel administrative offices) and formation personnel, presentations (oral and audio-visual) on the charism and tradition of the institutes, inter-community visits, joint times of recollection retreat or vacation, informal discussions and dialogues, study of substance and style of constitutions and proper law, and sharing personnel openings. An important part of the process at this stage is to give the members of the institute an opportunity to express their fears and expectations regarding a union or merger.

After the institutes have engaged in all the processes that help them to know and understand themselves, each other, the process of union or merger and the expected result, then members of each of the institutes should determine whether to proceed further. This may be accomplished by consultation with the membership, even a consultative vote.

If the institutes decide to proceed, the next step is to continue the previous procedures that were helpful in bringing the institutes together while beginning to develop a plan for merger or union that will be submitted to each institute and to the Congregation. In many cases at this stage a visitation is made to the members of the institute which initiated the process to hear their opinion and inform them of their rights. The visitor is often appointed by the diocesan bishop of the initiating institute.

After a plan for merger or union has been developed, it should be approved by each institute. The Congregation is flexible in regard to the method of approval depending on the size and organization of each institute. A "secret formal vote" is required of the members of the amalgamating institute (see no. 7 of the Congregation's letter), and permits the receiving institute to approve at a chapter or special assembly or in large institutes by the general superior and council and the provincial superiors and councils, or an enlarged general council. Each institute should carefully determine the method that best allows its membership to express its opinion.

The petition of the Congregation should summarize the reasons for the petition and specifically but briefly outline the entire process, the votation of the institutes and any important decisions unique to the particular petition such as which institutes' constitutions will be used even temporarily (for a union). In addition, the petition may include a proposed timetable for establishing a unified government which may be based on the preparation and execution of new civil law documents, financial and property transactions, and insurance coverage. This allows the canonical merger or union to be coordinated with the civil law structure. The petition should be supported by appropriate documentation that provides specific information on each institute, its members, its present situation and the plan for merger or union.

V. THE DECREE OF THE CONGREGATION

The decrees of the Congregation contain language common to most mergers and unions as well as language specific to a particular merger or union. The common language covers the protection of the rights of the members and the property of the institute. The decree often states the members remain in the same situation of religious profession as they are at the present; however, they are free to transfer to another institute or seek secularization. Depending on the situation, some decrees also require that members freely and willingly sign a document declaring they wish to be enrolled in the new institute.

In regard to property, the decrees provide that the property, rights and obligations of each of the institutes are to be registered in the name of the receiving institute or the new institute. Special forms of property such as property received for a particular purpose or with a condition of its use or property in which other parties have an interest or right must be treated in a manner that respects the rights or intentions of donors, testators or co-owners.

Specific elements in a decree may respond to matters contained in the petition such as the plan for interim government. Sometimes a decree will specify the manner of representation on an interim council until a merged or unified institute holds elections.

Members of institutes who do not wish to be members of the merged or united institute individually petition for transfer or secularization. These cases are processed in accord with the canons applying to transfer or departure. The decree of merger or union does not of itself provide for transfer or departure.

VI. IMPLEMENTING THE DECREE

When the decree of the Congregation is received, the institutes may begin putting into effect all that is required by the decree plus all the practical steps that result in merger or union. Depending on the institutes this may happen quickly or it may require a period of time. For more complicated mergers or unions it is helpful to indicate the time it will take to complete the merger or union. It takes time to restructure, plan elections, transfer property (if necessary), and rearrange finances. Usually a decree should be read in accord with the petition made by the institutes because the language is often responsive to the information originally sent to the

Congregation. Sometimes, language in decrees that may seem confusing is clear when read in the context of the original petition.

Usually, a decree is effective when received and accepted by the institutes. In some cases, however, the decree may specify the time and manner of acceptance such as "promulgation in the presence of a Special General Chapter."

VII. Conclusion

Institutes considering merger or union should approach the matter with great sensitivity. The preparation and the process must be carefully planned. There should be a clear understanding of the implications of the decision for the future as well as the options available to each member. The spiritual and psychological trauma that can result from any uprooting that may occur requires serious attention. Ongoing communication among leadership, between leadership groups, and between leadership and members is a necessity. If these factors are given proper consideration, merger or union can be life-giving for religious institutes.

Melanie Bair, O.S.F.
Jordan Hite, T.O.R.

This article originally appeared in *Bulletin on Issues of Religious Law*, Vol. 3, 1987.

13.
DEALING WITH THE DIFFICULT RELIGIOUS

I. INTRODUCTION

Members of the Church called to dedicate themselves to the glory of God and the service of others in consecrated life share a special gift or charism which unites them as a special family in Christ. In this community they support one another through concern and assistance and thus offer an example of universal reconciliation in Christ to the broader Church (cf. *Perfectae caritatis* 15; c. 602).

In institutes of religious life, this call to community is lived in common (c. 607, §2). Community life is strengthened and witnessed through sharing a common religious house, liturgical or communal prayer, meals, recreation, and temporal goods. Superiors of religious institutes are called to foster community life in common with the other members of the institute and to meet the personal needs of the members in a suitable manner (c. 619). A religious has both the right and obligation of community life in common, and cannot be absent from the religious house without the permission of the superior. Likewise, the religious cannot be absent for a lengthy period of time without a just reason and the permission of the major superior given with the consent of the council (c. 665, §1).

Given the right and obligation of each member of a religious institute to live community life in common, a problem arises with the person we may call, for the want of a better term, the difficult religious. At times, a member of a religious institute willfully or inadvertently disturbs the peace and tranquillity of community life. This member's behavior destroys the harmony needed for the living out of the charism of the institute, and the other members find it difficult, if not impossible, to live and support one another in the disordered community. The words, actions and demeanor of the religious mar the tranquillity of the local house and violate the rights of the other members.

II. INTERVENTION

Since the obligation of superiors in religious life is to foster the charism of the institute, the local superior is the initial person to deal with this member. Patience and compassion should be expended on the member finding serious difficulty in the religious life. The person should be led to see through examples that his/her aberrant behavior precludes the harmonious living out of the charism of the institute. Specific modification of behavior patterns should be recommended, and counseling should be offered. The immediate superior should be knowledgeable regarding psychologists and psychiatrists who, in addition to their professional expertise, possess a reasonable knowledge of religious life. Many dioceses have the resource of a counseling service which offers such skilled personnel.

If counseling is refused and the disruptive behavior continues, the member should be advised by the local or immediate superior that the major superior (general or provincial) will be informed of the behavior pattern detrimental to the community life of the local house. The values prompting such recourse to higher authority are the good of the individual religious and the right of the other members to live in the spirit of their institute. Too often in the past, the difficult religious was neglected under the guise of charity to the detriment of justice to the other members attempting to live out their vocation. There is no charity unless it is rooted in justice, and major superiors have the serious responsibility of protecting the rights and pointing to the obligations of all those incorporated into the institute through religious profession. Sometimes, an individual member forgets and must be reminded that membership in a religious institute, like all memberships, brings obligations with rights.

III. Leave of Absence

It is important that the local or major superior encourage the member experiencing difficulty to get a thorough physical examination. Aberrant behavior can at times be traced to chemical imbalances in the body which frequently accompany illness or mid-life transition. At times, prescribed medication greatly alleviates the chemical imbalance and resultant atypical behavior of the religious. If the behavior results from mental or emotional illness, or from alcohol or drug abuse, it becomes necessary for the religious to receive treatment in a hospital or rehabilitation facility. The major superior (general or provincial) with the consent of the council can grant the member a leave from the religious house for such treatment as long as is necessary (c. 665, §1). If the religious with difficulty is a nun, the diocesan bishop has the faculty with consent of the superior of the monastery to permit the nun to leave the cloister for the necessary period of time (c. 667, §4). The member on leave is accountable to the superior and should follow the obligations of religious life to the best of his/her ability while away from the community. The major superior, or one delegated by the same superior, should keep in contact with the religious on leave and with the professional(s) treating the problem so as to understand the progress and the member's continued ability to live community life. An unmonitored leave of absence, apart from the one described wherein the troubled religious receives medical attention and counseling, prolongs the problem of the member and fails to address the resultant disorder in local community life.

IV. Exclaustration

When the local superior advises the major superior of the serious behavioral problem of the difficult member, all that is possible should be done at the higher level in the way of exhortation, counseling, testing and even changes in residence and ministry to effect remedial behavior. It is not unusual in such cases that the problem arises from the incompatibility of the personality of the religious with that of the local superior or one or more of the other members.

While apostolic institutes have numerous local houses to place such a member, the contemplative institutes are limited in this regard. However, a temporary transfer to another monastery of the same institute may be helpful in resolving the problem. The temporary transfer could lead to a permanent one for the benefit of all concerned (c. 684, §3). The important considerations are the good of the troubled religious and the religious communities involved. In such cases, the honest communication between the major and local superiors involved is an essential element.

If a disruptive behavior pattern continues after the interventions of the local and major superiors, exclaustration may be the answer for a member having no mental or emotional illness, or in the case of illness, refusing professional treatment. Likewise, exclaustration may be the solution for a religious receiving counseling, when in the opinion of the professional(s), community life serves only to increase the stress of the disturbed member. Exclaustration may be voluntary, enforced, or for the duration of necessity.

A. Voluntary Exclaustration

At times, a difficult religious comes to a realization through the observations of superiors and the counseling of professionals in the behavioral sciences that community life puts too great a demand on his/her human frailty. In such cases, the religious may approach the major superior and request a time of exclaustration in order to evaluate his/her capacity to continue in religious life. The general superior with the consent of the council can grant the member an indult of exclaustration for a period of up to three years. The Apostolic See grants the indult of exclaustration for cloistered nuns (c. 686, §§1-2).

The religious on voluntary exclaustration is free to return to the religious institute at any time. If it seems necessary to extend the exclaustration beyond three years, the petition of the religious and the supporting statement of the major superior are sent to the Apostolic See in institutes of pontifical right or to the diocesan bishop in institutes of diocesan right (c. 686, §1).

B. Involuntary or Enforced Exclaustration

It may be that the difficult religious fails to grasp the gravity of the effects of his/her behavior; i.e., the disruption of community life and the violation of the rights of the other members in the institute. Or it may be that recognizing the same, the member obstinately refuses to modify his/her conduct or to request voluntary exclaustration. If community life has and continues to be imperiled by the religious' behavior, and the competent superior has exhausted all suitable remedies, the major superior may be obliged to begin the process of enforced exclaustration for both the benefit of the member and the good of the other members. Enforced exclaustration is a grave measure and should only be employed when all other reasonable efforts have ended in failure.

If the major superior is a provincial superior, it is wise to apprise the general superior of the seriousness of the situation well in advance of presenting him/her with the documents for the enforced exclaustration. Too often, poor communication between the general and provincial superior results in the inability of the general superior to comprehend the full impact of the grave problem at the provincial level. Poor communication may even serve to cause friction and a lack of cooperation between the general and provincial superiors called to nurture the unity of the institute.

The immediate major superior should meet with the religious in the presence of the assistant or vicar and state that the continued aberrant behavior is a serious threat to the community life of the religious institute. The major superior should present to the religious in writing the problems and the imperatives necessary to remedy the behavior patterns. Likewise, the written directive should contain the statement that failure to comply with the mandate will result in enforced exclaustration. A suitable period of time (fifteen to ninety days) should be given the religious to modify his/her conduct, and any defense offered by the religious should be carefully recorded. If the religious fails within the given time frame to comply with the mandates, a second warning is given. If after the suitable period of time, this second warning proves ineffectual, the general superior with the consent of the council can request enforced exclaustration for the member from the Apostolic See or the diocesan bishop in the case of a diocesan institute (c. 686, §2).

All of the acts of the case (warnings, defense, statement of the provincial or general superior, an account of the behavioral problems and applied remedies together with curriculum vitae of the religious) should be sent to the authority having the power to grant the enforced exclaustration. It is to be noted that the procedure for enforced exclaustration is similar to that for facultative dismissal (cc. 697-700). This procedure is recommended so that proper documentation is available in the event the religious appeals the decision (*CLD* 9: 458-460).

C. Exclaustration for the Duration Of Necessity

The practice of the Congregation for Institutes of Consecrated and Societies of Apostolic Life (CICLSAL) has been to grant an indult of exclaustration for the duration of necessity to a religious with psychological disturbance. This exclaustration can be voluntary, i.e., at the request of the ill member who recognizes his/her inability to live the religious life. The procedure can be comforting to a disturbed member who cherishes the spirituality of the institute and the vowed commitment, but finds community life increasingly more difficult to live. Exclaustration for the duration of necessity can be imposed by CICLSAL at the request of the superior general with the consent of the council. This would happen if the religious refuses to request the exclaustration, and the behavior patterns resulting from the mental or emotional illness cause grave disruption of religious community life. In such cases, the imposed exclaustration is not a disciplinary measure, but a dispensation to live outside the religious institute for reasons of health. It is a way of assisting both the troubled religious and the other members of the institute. The rescript states that the religious may return to the institute when he/she has recovered sufficiently. It would seem that the expert opinion of the professional(s) caring for the member should be obtained both in the case of a member on voluntary exclaustration and the one on involuntary exclaustration petitioning CICLSAL for reentry.

D. Effects of Exclaustration

The following are the effects of exclaustration for the member of a religious institute as stated in canon 687. The religious:

> a) is dispensed from those obligations which are incompatible with the new condition of life;
>
> b) remains dependent on and under the care of the superiors of the institute and the local ordinary;
>
> c) may wear the religious habit unless the indult specifies otherwise;
>
> d) lacks active and passive voice.

The indult of exclaustration dispenses the member from such obligations as the horarium for prayer, meals, and the other community activities. The major superior or delegate should organize some means of accountability for the religious on exclaustration. Periodic contacts through phone calls, letters, and personal meetings reflect the interest of the institute for its members while reminding the exclaustrated religious of the seriousness of this time of reflection and adaptation. Too often there is neither communication to nor from the exclaustrated member, and the member experiences alienation, loneliness, isolation, and fear.

It is correct and courteous for the major superior to apprise the local ordinary of the place wherein the exclaustrated religious will reside. The member may need someone to discuss his/her vocation to the religious institute or acclimation to a secular life, and many dioceses have personnel competent and experienced to assist the religious. The local ordinary should express every concern for exclaustrated religious in the diocese seeking his pastoral care.

While the religious habit may be worn, it seems in most instances that the option not to wear the habit is the practice. This is probably the more prudent choice, inasmuch as questions are frequently raised when a habited religious lives alone in an apartment. Likewise, many exclaustrated religious seek employment beyond the ministries of the Church.

The loss of active and passive voice is not a punitive measure. Rather, this provision in the law respects the need of the religious and the purpose of exclaustration. A person seriously reflecting on his/her life's direction cannot give full attention to the issues and concerns of a chapter nor accept an office of responsibility in the institute.

When a member leaves on exclaustration, some monetary provision is given in keeping with equity and charity (c. 607, §2). It is important to understand that the exclaustrated religious is truly a member of the institute with rights and obligations. If the member cannot provide adequately for himself/herself, the religious institute is obliged to do so. It would be important both for the institute and the member that the exclaustrated religious be kept on the health plan of the institute until there is assurance that he/she has coverage through employment. Some institutes provide interest-free loans for the member, and the religious reimburses the institute as his/her financial situation stabilizes. While many exclaustrated religious find gainful employment, the mentally or emotionally ill religious often finds difficulty in procuring or keeping a position. The religious institute should assist the member spiritually, morally, and materially. Sometimes it is necessary to help the religious find work adapted to his/her capacity. In such instances where advanced age or psychological frailty are factors, the institute should through a written contract work out financial assistance for the needy member. What must be remembered is that these exclaustrated religious are truly members of the religious institute.

V. Dismissal

The process for dismissal should be begun only after every other means such as exhortation, counseling, changes in residence and ministry have been employed to assist the difficult member. The procedure should never be applied to those members suffering from emotional or mental illness, or who are advanced in age. In such cases, exclaustration whether voluntary, involuntary, or for the duration of necessity should be the procedure.

Since we are speaking of grave misconduct which seriously disrupts community life over a significant period of time, we exclude from our discussion the automatic or *ipso facto* dismissal of canon 694, and the mandatory dismissal of canon 695. The facultative dismissal of canon 696 which addresses the problem of the difficult member reads:

> 1. A member can also be dismissed for other causes provided that they are grave, external, imputable and juridically proven, such as: habitual neglect of the obligations of consecrated life; repeated violations of the sacred bonds; pertinacious disobedience to lawful prescriptions of superiors in a serious matter; grave scandal arising from the culpable behavior of the member; pertinacious upholding or spreading of doctrines condemned by the magisterium or atheism; unlawful absence mentioned in canon 665, §2 lasting six months; other causes of similar seriousness which may be determined by the proper law of the institute.
>
> 2. Even causes of lesser seriousness determined in proper law suffice for the dismissal of a member in temporary vows.

If the aberrant behavior of the member does not change after repeated assistance and support, the major superior should meet with the religious, point out the incongruity of the behavior with religious life and encourage the difficult religious to seek an indult of departure from religious life. If the religious refuses to seek an indult of departure, the major superior, after consulting the council, may commence the dismissal process. The process according to canons 697-700 should be followed meticulously. In writing or before two witnesses the major superior should warn the member that failure to remedy the grave violations will result in dismissal. The member should be given opportunity for defense and a period of time from at least fifteen to ninety days to show improvement. If this first warning is ineffectual, a second warning should be given after the time period has elapsed with both the opportunity for defense and the same span of time for remedial efforts in behavior.

If the two warnings fail to produce any improvement in the behavioral pattern of the individual, the major superior, after the time has elapsed, is to sign the acts along with the notary and send them to the general superior. Here again, it is important that the general superior be made aware of the problem and the efforts to assist the member beforehand, so as not to shock nor surprise. The religious can communicate directly with the general superior.

The general superior and council, which must consist of four members for validity, study the acts of the case and the defense of the member. If by a secret collegial vote they decide to dismiss the religious, a decree is drawn up. For validity, the decree must express the reasons in the law and in fact for the dismissal and the right of the religious dismissed to have recourse to the competent authority within ten days of the notification. The recourse has a suspensive effect on the dismissal. The decree, however, has no effect unless it is confirmed by the Holy See after the acts are forwarded or in the case of a diocesan institute, by the bishop in whose diocese is the house to which the religious is assigned (cc. 697-700). The diocesan bishop decides on dismissal for a member of an autonomous monastery after receiving the acts of the case reviewed by the council (c. 699, §2).

The one legitimately dismissed from a religious institute cannot claim anything from the institute for work done while a member. However, the institute should show equity and charity in dealing with such a member (c. 702). Even in this case, the major superior as the representative of the institute should see that the dismissed religious has monetary assistance at departure. While such a person is legitimately separated from the institute, it would be wise, practical and charitable to keep the dismissed religious covered by the health benefits of the institute until he/she obtains gainful employment with such benefits. Frequently a dismissed member leaves angry, but time, experience and reflection often bring healing and the awareness of the person's inadequacy to live as a religious. The spiritual and moral support of the institute should not be denied such a person.

Concluding Observations

Being an overview, this paper does not address all of the behavioral problems which prevent one from living a committed religious life. Besides the religious whose conduct disrupts community life, the nominal religious could well be the subject of another paper. Such a person lives religious life within the juridic limits of the institute without significant personal development nor positive contribution to the life and growth of the religious community. The nominal religious lives an unexamined life and becomes like deadwood on the tree or darnel in the wheat. This member, too, merits the concern and assistance of major superiors. Often the religious' passive existence in community life serves as an excuse for superiors to avoid taking effective action on behalf of the nominal religious.

Dealing with a religious after serious behavioral patterns have continued over a significant period of time proves onerous for the superiors, the members of the religious community and the problem religious. Such a sensitive and draining procedure can be alleviated and even avoided through wise policies in the admission, formation, and ongoing formation programs in the religious institute.

Despite the scarcity of vocations, there should be a careful scrutiny of applicants to a religious institute, particularly today in light of the instability in families and society. Likewise, the competent superior admitting a religious in a transfer process from another religious institute should require an evaluation from the major superior of the former institute. In both instances, major superiors should be faithful to the norms of canon 642 in the admission process. The careful screening of applicants, though not infallible, will help avoid the presence of persons with potential personality problems which may worsen as time goes on.

Formation personnel have the grave obligations of observing and evaluating the personality and performance of those in initial formation and their capacity to live the life of the religious institute. Regrettable at times, emphasis in formation is placed on a pseudo-spiritual life far removed from the practical demands of community life. The failure to integrate the spiritual and psychological often leads to frustration later. It takes wisdom and common sense on the part of formation personnel to make a prudential judgment on the suitability of a candidate to continue in a lifestyle where community living is an essential element.

Through pastoral visitations and beneficial programs, the major superiors fulfill their serious obligations of nurturing and supporting the members in living the charism of the institute. No means should be spared to encourage a healthy and holy lifestyle which contributes both to the Christian human development of the members and those they serve in the ministry of the Church. Behavioral problems of individuals should be addressed early on both for the good of the individual and the other members. If left unchallenged, these aberrations become accepted as normal modes of conduct and contribute seriously to the weakening of the religious spirit in the institute. While religious have rights through profession and subsequent incorporation in their religious institutes, they likewise have serious obligations of contributing to the life and holiness of the other members and to the people of God through the fostering of the grace of their own vocation.

It is important that some record of grave behavioral problems be kept in the personnel files of the religious institute. Often a major superior falls heir to problems which have been escalating over a long period of years. The conscientious superior, recognizing the harm done to both the individual religious and the local community, frequently has no recourse to a record of the disruptive behavioral pattern of the individual. It is difficult, if not impossible, for the present competent authority to reconstruct accurately an account of the member's misconduct in the institute over an extended period. Charity is rooted in justice, and there is no charity to the difficult religious nor to the other members of the community when serious problems are left unaddressed and unresolved. In such an institute, there will be a gradual weakening of the vibrancy and enthusiasm of the religious for their personal and communal growth in Christ.

Rose McDermott, S.S.J.

This article originally appeared in *Bulletin on Issues of Religious Law*, Vol. 3, 1987.

14.
Transfer to Another Institute – Canons 684-685

I. Introduction

Canons 684 and 685 of the 1983 Code of Canon Law give the bare bones of the canonical process for a religious in perpetual profession transferring from a religious institute to another religious institute. There are significant considerations inextricably bound up with this decision that merit attention of the religious who considers a transfer and the persons who assist in this canonical process. This short article will attempt to raise these issues as well as review the canonical norms which must be observed for such a re-orientation of one's vocation.

II. Reason for Transfer

It is important both for the religious transferring and for the counselor, superior or friend in whom the religious confides to determine the reason or attraction that draws the person to another religious institute. Since we are speaking here of a religious in perpetual profession, the person has been formed in a particular spirituality and way of life. A certain charism, history and patrimony have helped shape this person over a period of years. Other members of the institute have lived and shared these values with the person. Hopefully, there would be a strong attraction to another institute and set of values that will necessarily compensate for those relinquished with the departure from the former institute. There should be a healthy predisposition to the new life direction deliberated on in prayer and wise counsel. A transfer should resemble the initial response to vocation, a strong attraction to the charism of an institute manifested in the witness and lives of the members with an equally strong desire to unite one's life and energies to this particular gift of the Spirit for the life and holiness of the Church.

There are times when major superiors, vicars for religious, spiritual directors or counselors interview a religious in perpetual profession who expresses an intention to transfer only to discover that the person harbors a great deal of bitterness or resentment for the initial institute and its members, with no resolution of the difficulties. The tensions arise from problems with persons in authority, ministry placement or significant elements of community life lived in common. Determination to transfer under such difficulties with no particular attraction for another institute seems more like an escape from present unpleasant circumstances. If such be the case, the person will not be at peace nor disposed to enter into the spirit of a new lifestyle with the enthusiasm and joy that should accompany a decision to intensify one's Christian life. One wonders, too, about the justice to the new institute if a person transfers bearing such unresolved problems and difficulties. If a religious is beset and upset with problems and has no particular attraction to another charism, it is better either to resolve the problems within the initial institute or to move out for a period of voluntary exclaustration (c. 686, §§1, 2) in order to resolve such issues and to heal before seeking a new life direction.

There may seem to be irreconcilable differences between the member and the initial institute. At times the member sincerely believes that he or she can no longer grow as a fully mature human being within the context of the present lifestyle. This has to be dealt with, and the member has to realistically determine if the attraction to another religious institute will fulfill expectations. Religious life has two essential elements, the public profession of the counsels and community life lived in common according to the proper law of the institute (c. 607, §2). A person with serious problems in one religious institute, particularly around these two essential elements, should be aware how these essential elements are lived according to the proper law of the new institute before proceeding with the transfer process.

III. Procedure

The religious in perpetual vows cannot transfer to another religious institute without the permission of the supreme moderator of each institute given with the consent of their respective councils (c. 684, §1). Since the general superior of a religious institute has, as a sacred trust, the good of the members, it would seem permission to transfer could not be given, or at best given with reservations, if unresolved difficulties around the very essentials of religious life were apparent in the life of the member. In large institutes with provinces, the input of the provincial superior is most important. In justice, difficulties in the essentials of religious life should be brought to the attention of the member, and he or she should be made to realize that these same difficulties will most assuredly arise in the new institute. The superior general of the receiving institute should request an evaluation of the petitioner from the superior general of the initial institute, and an honest appraisal should be given. This recommendation should be shared with the council before their consent is sought.

IV. Probationary Period and Effects of Transfer

The probationary period prior to perpetual profession for the religious transferring must consist of a period of at least three years. There may be a longer period required by the proper law of the institute, but it is not good to prolong the time of probation unduly. During this period, the person remains a religious with vows, but the rights and obligations in the former institute are suspended. He or she is obliged to obey the superiors and directors of the receiving institute during this probationary period. The transferring religious has neither active nor passive voice in either the former nor present institute.

The transfer process is a two-edged sword, and the receiving institute should have an experienced religious, preferably a formation director, in charge of the transferring religious. The period of probation is a time of decision for both the new institute and for the religious. It is a time to see if the human qualities and aspirations of the candidate resonate with those identified in the receiving institute. This decision is made mutually by the institute in the person of the superior competent in the proper law of the institute and by the person transferring. This religious can petition to make perpetual profession in the new institute, return to his or her former institute or petition for a time of exclaustration or perpetual separation from the initial institute. Likewise, the person with authority in the new institute can make a decision after consultation with the council and formation personnel that the personal vocation of the transferee does not reflect the charism of the new institute. Canon 684, §2 speaks of return to the former institute or definitive departure; however, this in no way precludes a period of exclaustration from the initial institute according to the norms of law. Likewise, if the person decides to return to the former institute, she or he cannot be prevented from so doing.

Financial considerations are absent from the norms on transfer. Concerns such as health coverage and board during the three years of probation would have to be worked out according to the policies of the two religious institutes. With perpetual profession in the new religious institute, the person's patrimony, act of cession and will would have to be adjusted in accordance with the rights and obligations of the transferred religious and the new institute according to its proper law.

V. Conclusion

This short article has dealt with the transfer of a religious in perpetual profession from his or her institute to another religious institute, since this is by far the more common type of transfer. However, there are also the following types of transfers.

> 1. A religious transferring from an autonomous monastery to another of the same institute, federation or confederation. Here it is sufficient to have the consent of the major superior of both monasteries and the chapter of the receiving monastery. Proper law is to be observed, and a new profession is not required (c. 684, §3).

> 2. A religious in perpetual profession transferring to a secular institute or a society of apostolic life or a member definitively incorporated in either of the latter two canonical institutes transferring to a religious institute. In such cases, the permission of the Holy See is required, and its mandates are to be observed (c. 684, §5).

Finally, there is no provision in the Code of Canon Law for a transfer from a canonical institute to a non-canonical group. In such cases, the religious in perpetual profession or the member definitively incorporated into a canonical institute would have to procure an indult of departure before joining such an association.

Rose McDermott, S.S.J.

This article originally appeared in *Bulletin on Issues of Religious Law*, Vol. 5, 1989.

15.
RELATIONSHIP BETWEEN BISHOPS AND RELIGIOUS: MUTUAL RIGHTS AND DUTIES

I. INTRODUCTORY COMMENTS

The topic at hand is a vast one which might be better understood by beginning with two current canonical principles regarding bishops and religious. First, it is clear that any diocesan bishop possesses all the ordinary, proper, and immediate power required for the exercise of his pastoral ministry in the diocese entrusted to his care (c. 381, §1), and that he also has general pastoral responsibility for and oversight of — among other things — all the faithful, all teaching and preaching, and all sacramental and liturgical celebrations (cc. 383, §1; 386, §1; and 387). Second, religious institutes pertain to the life and sanctity of the Church (cc. 573-574) and, when legitimately established as juridic persons, they possess a rightful autonomy by which they can follow their own internal discipline as well as preserve and protect their institute's "patrimony," that is: the nature, purpose, spirit, character, and sound traditions associated with their institute (cc. 586 and 578).

In connection with the first principle, the diocesan bishop can conduct a visitation of all churches and oratories habitually attended by the faithful as well as a visitation of schools and other spiritual or temporal works of religion or charity entrusted to religious (c. 683, §1), and — simultaneously — all religious are subject to the authority of the diocesan bishop in matters concerning the care of souls, public worship and works of the apostolate in a particular diocese (c. 578, §1). In connection with the second principle, the proper law of each institute is supposed to articulate the fundamental elements of life and discipline for its members (c. 587) and each member is urged to order his or her life according to these requirements (c. 598, §2), while — simultaneously — all religious institutes and their members always exist in relation to the universal Church and to particular dioceses and are always in some way subject to competent ecclesiastical authorities external to the institute (cc. 576; 590-591; and 593-594).

Two additional important points need to be kept in mind in relation to this topic. First, whatever the universal law may say about the relative roles of bishops and religious, the approved proper law of a particular institute (i.e., the "rule" or "constitutions") always takes precedence over universal law even if that proper law is contrary to it. Second, regardless of the canonical rules concerning bishops and religious throughout church history, this same history provides ample witness to the fact that finding and/or maintaining a proper balance in the relationship between bishops and religious have often been delicate and elusive tasks, as well as not entirely successful ones.

II. Canonical Categories

Under the 1983 Code there are several ways to categorize religious institutes, but these canonical categories are not mutually exclusive nor do they in any way actually exhaust the possibilities for the great variety of religious institutes that exist. However, it is helpful for our purposes to consider religious institutes as diocesan or pontifical, as apostolic or contemplative, and as lay or clerical. The former distinction of exempt and non-exempt religious institutes still exists in the 1983 Code (c. 591), but these terms as such are no longer used in reference to religious. Since the practical consequences of the distinction are relatively negligible at present because of other canonical requirements, exemption will not be addressed directly.

Diocesan institutes (often referred to as "diocesan right") are those which have been canonically established by a diocesan bishop and have not subsequently obtained juridic recognition from the Apostolic See (cc. 579; 589; and 594). Pontifical institutes (often referred to as "pontifical right") are those which have been canonically established by the Apostolic See or which have originated as a diocesan institute but subsequently obtained a formal decree of approbation from the Apostolic See (cc. 589 and 593). These categories are mutually exclusive, and it is relatively easy to determine canonically to which category any religious institute belongs.

Apostolic institutes are those dedicated to works of the apostolate in such a way that apostolic action is part of the nature of the institute itself (c. 675, §1), that is, part of its juridic patrimony as described in canon 578. Contemplative institutes are those dedicated to contemplation and are described canonically as somewhat in contrast to institutes that engage in apostolic activity (c. 674). This canonical distinction is neither accurate nor exhaustive since it neglects monastic institutes which engage in apostolic activity as part of their heritage (such as Benedictines with their long-recognized tradition of monastic schools) and it equally neglects institutes which by their nature are both contemplative and apostolic (such as Dominicans with their long-recognized tradition of contemplation flowing into action).

Lay institutes are those recognized as such by the Church whose purpose does not include the exercise of the sacrament of orders (cc. 588, §3 and 676), whereas clerical institutes are those recognized as such by the Church whose purpose includes the exercise of orders and which are governed by clerics (c. 588, §2). This distinction is generally correct and, though it appears in some respects to be juridically exhaustive and mutually exclusive, there is currently great debate about its genuine accuracy as well as about its practical adequacy for some religious institutes (such as for the various branches of Franciscan friars).

Finally, there is actually a canonical sub-category of contemplative/monastic religious institute that is nowhere defined in the code, but which is consistently mentioned and treated differently from all others. It consists in practice of *sui iuris* monasteries of nuns, that is, technically those independent houses of monastic women who profess solemn vows and observe papal enclosure (c. 667, §3), and which (houses) are subject to the special vigilance of the diocesan bishop by reason of canon 615.

III. Episcopal Responsibilities

The next logical step in attempting to explain the canonical relationships among bishops and religious is to identify the canons of the code which apply to religious and specifically mention the diocesan bishop, plus canons elsewhere that concern the diocesan bishop and specifically mention religious. If we begin sequentially with the general norms on consecrated life (cc. 573-606) and the specific canons concerning religious (cc. 607-709) and relate the canons on bishops to these, the areas of episcopal responsibility can be somewhat accurately categorized thus:

Establishing an institute	cc. 579; 589; 605
Respecting autonomy of institutes	c. 586
Approving constitutions	cc. 587, §1; 595
Special care or vigilance	cc. 594; 615
Establishing houses	cc. 609, §1; 611
Altering apostolate of a house	c. 612
Suppressing houses	cc. 616, §1
Presiding at elections	c. 625, §2
Visitation of institutes	cc. 628, §2; 397, §2
Confessors for (lay) institutes	c. 630, §3
Finance of institutes	cc. 637; 638, §4; 1266; 1291; 1292, §1; 1295
Admission of clerics	cc. 644; 645
Entrance into/exit from cloister	c. 667, §4
Exercise of apostolate(s)	cc. 672; 678, §§1 and 2
Coordination of apostolates	cc. 678, §3; 680
Works/contracts/eccl. office	cc. 681; 682
Visitation of apostolates	cc. 683, §1; 397, §2
Penalties applied to religious	cc. 679; 683, §2; 1320
Indult of exclaustration	cc. 686; 687
Indult of departure	cc. 688, §2; 691, §2; 693
Dismissal of religious	cc. 699, §2; 700; 701

If for practical purposes we divide the categories of religious institutes into diocesan, pontifical, and autonomous monasteries of the canon 615 type (i.e., for all practical purposes monasteries of nuns) and then combine this division with the above list, the involvement of bishops with respect to religious appears more specifically as indicated in the chart below. Parentheses in any column indicate an indirect reference to responsibility of the bishop or to involvement of the bishop that is known through the practice of the Roman curia. Thus, for example, in the category of "Finances of institutes" there is an (X) in the column for pontifical institutes because *de iure* (c. 638, §3) the diocesan bishop is not involved in alienation of property of such institutes but *de facto* requests sent by pontifical institutes to the Congregation for Institutes of Consecrated Life and Societies of Apostolic Life (CICLSAL) for permission to alienate property are not successfully processed unless they include the diocesan bishop's opinion regarding the proposed transaction. Similarly, in the category of "Exercise of apostolates" there is an (X) in the column for monasteries of canon 615 because *de facto* these are most often monasteries of nuns with papal enclosures who exercise no external apostolates, although de iure canon 615 is not restricted to only monasteries of nuns.

	PONTIFICAL INSTITUTES	DIOCESAN INSTITUTES	MONASTERIES OF CANON 615
Establishing an institute cc. 579; 589; 605		X	(X)
Respecting autonomy c. 586	X	X	X
Approving constitutions cc. 587, §1: 595		X	
Special care or vigilance cc. 594; 615		X	X
Establishing houses cc. 609, §1; 611	X	X	X
Altering apostolate of houses c. 612	X	X	
Suppressing houses cc. 616, §1	X	X	X
Presiding at elections c. 625, §2		X	X
Visitation of institutes cc. 628, §2; 397, §2		X	X

	Pontifical Institutes	Diocesan Institutes	Monasteries of Canon 615
Confessors for (lay) institutes c. 630, §3	X	X	X
Finances of Institutes cc. 637; 638, §4; 1266; 1291; 1292, §1; 1295	(X)	X	X
Admission of clerics cc. 644; 645	X	X	
Entrance into/exit from cloister c. 667; §4 (of nuns)			X
Exercise of apostolate(s) cc. 672; 678, §§1 and 2	X	X	(X)
Coordination of apostolates cc. 678, §3; 680	X	X	(X)
Works/contracts/eccl. office cc. 681; 682	X	X	(X)
Visitation of apostolates cc. 683, §1; 397, §2	X	X	(X)
Penalties applied to religious cc. 679; 683, §2; 1320	X	X	X
Indult of exclaustration cc. 686; 687		X	
Indult of departure cc. 688, §2; 691, §2; 693		X	X
Dismissal of religious cc. 699, §2; 700; 701		X	X

IV. Diocesan Institutes and Pontifical Institutions

It should be clear from the above chart that the diocesan bishop relates to both diocesan and pontifical institutes but that his responsibilities are far more extensive for diocesan institutes. For diocesan institutes, the diocesan bishop approves their constitutions as well as subsequent changes made in them, dispenses from these constitutions in particular cases, handles matters of major import beyond the power of the institute's internal authorities, presides at elections of the supreme moderator, is responsible for visitation of the institute and its members, has the right to be informed of the institute's finances, gives consent for (some) alienation of property, grants indults of exclaustration and departure, and confirms decrees of dismissal.

For pontifical institutes, on the other hand, the diocesan bishop's involvement is limited primarily to matters regarding houses of the institute (i.e., to any *domus religiosa* in the technical sense) and to the exercise of any apostolate by members of a religious institute in his diocese. Religious houses and the apostolate(s) exercised by religious are directly related by canon 611, which states unequivocally that consent of the diocesan bishop to establish a house of the institute in any diocese includes the right: 1) to live the life of the institute in that house, 2) to exercise the proper apostolate of the institute in and from that house; and 3) for clerical institutes, to have a church and carry out sacred ministry therein.

A religious house in the technical sense is a permanent residence for members of the institute which has been established according to the requirements of law (cc. 609-610) and wherein the life of the institute according to its proper law is observed in a stable and on-going manner. If there is no technical house established by an institute in a particular diocese, then technically speaking the rights of canon 611 as indicated above simply do not obtain for members of the institute who live and exercise an apostolate in that diocese. In such cases — i.e., where there is no house of the institute legitimately established — any religious who exercises an apostolate there does so under the authority of and at the discretion of the diocesan bishop in all matters relating to that apostolate.

V. Ministry Considerations in a Diocese

There are several generic canonical categories or types of apostolic activity which may be exercised by religious in a diocese. The type of apostolic activity that is most removed from any involvement on the part of the diocesan bishop is that which is totally internal to an institute of pontifical right, for example, a house of studies operated by a pontifical institute exclusively for the education of its own members, such as for novices or those in initial formation (c. 683, §1). Interference in these endeavors of religious institutes would be a direct violation of the autonomy mentioned in and juridically protected by canon 586. On the other hand, all apostolates owned and/or operated by religious as collective (or "corporate") endeavors of the institute but which are frequented by the faithful of the diocese on a regular basis are subject to episcopal visitation (c. 683, §1) as well as to appropriate action by the bishop in order to correct any abuses that may come to his attention if the superior of the institute has been warned about them to no avail (c. 683, §2).

If a particular ministry is entrusted to a religious institute by the diocesan bishop (such as a diocesan high school or orphanage, etc.), carefully constructed, mutually agreeable written contracts should be concluded between the diocesan bishop (or his official representative) and the competent authority of the religious institute (or his or her official representative). These contracts should include the nature of the work to be done, the means of filling the positions), and standard remuneration for the work done (c. 681). If individual religious are employed by a diocese to fulfill a particular ministry, similar contracts should be made in order to protect the institute and the diocese, as well as the religious in question. Moreover, if the position held by a religious in a diocese is technically an ecclesiastical office (c. 145), such as pastor of a parish, etc., then this should be clearly indicated in the contractual arrangement with provision added for removal of the religious from office with simultaneous termination of the contract at the initiative of either the bishop or the religious superior in accord with canon 682.

There is a good deal of confusion in practice regarding the ministry or apostolate or work of many religious today. There are two basic contributors to this confusion. First, in theory any apostolate of a religious institute which is proper to that institute or part of its institutional patrimony should be appropriately specified in its fundamental documents (cc. 578; 587, §1; and 675, §1) and then there should be little question as to whether a member is exercising a ministry or function proper to the institute. So, for example, if education were an apostolate proper to a particular religious institute, a member might engage in this apostolate within the institute in an educational facility belonging to one's own religious community or entrusted by the diocese to that religious community or even in an educational facility owned or entrusted to another religious community, and he or she would still be exercising an apostolate proper to the institute. Second, in order to engage in ministries or offices outside of those proper to the institute, specific permission of one's legitimate superior is technically required (c. 672).

However, it is often difficult to ascertain clearly what precisely are the works proper to a particular institute because these are often expressed in the fundamental documents in very general terms, such as: "Our purpose is to carry the works of mercy to the needy of our society." Consequently, it is often quite unclear as to what actually constitutes works which are not proper to the institute, and the question then becomes: What in fact might a religious do in a diocese — in the line of apostolic activity — that would not fit the above description? In addition, there is often not a clear delineation in institutes or in dioceses of what functions and positions actually constitute (ecclesiastical) offices in the technical sense (c. 145).

What can be affirmed with some certainty, however, is that there is no such thing as a purely private apostolate in the Church. Any religious who engages in any formal activity that carries out a ministry or office or function or activity relating directly to the building up of the Church and the salvation of the world (c. 573) in any technical and formal manner is involved in an apostolic activity governed by canons

75

673-683. It can also be affirmed with some certainty that religious may engage in many activities because of temporary or long-term necessity or temporary or long-term personal choice and which are permitted by one's religious superiors, but that these are not apostolic activities per se and are not governed by any of the canonical regulations thereof. So, for example, if a religious for some period of time engages with appropriate permission in a meaningful income-producing (or non-income-producing) independent activity, such as a department store clerk or a bank teller or a travel agent or a systems analyst for a computer company, these cannot be construed as apostolic activities in the technical meaning of the term.

VI. Some Concluding Comments

Finally, regarding the apostolic relationship between bishops and religious, it must be admitted there is a complexus of qualified obligations and rights on the part of both bishops and of religious institutes, as well as of members themselves which cannot ever totally be encompassed by legal directives. Two related aspects of the bishop/religious apostolic relationship are worthy of note here. These are: the right of any religious (indeed, of any Christian) to his or her privacy and good name (c. 220); and the genuine need — which must be balanced with the above right — for any competent authority to be adequately informed in employing or conferring an office on a religious as to whether or not he or she is truly suitable for that position (cc. 145, §2; 149).

It is perhaps not too bold to suggest that religious institutes in the past may have been all too eager to "re-cycle" troublesome religious to this or that apostolate in an unsuspecting diocese (or parish or school or hospital) with apparently little or no regard for anything other than convenient and minimally contentious relocation of seriously problematic members. On the other hand, it is apparently not uncommon currently for diocesan officials to request from religious superiors personal information about members of the institute who wish to serve in their diocese. Often enough this requested information can be of such a nature that superiors are not legally free to share it (either canonically or civilly) with anyone inside or outside the institute without the express permission of the religious in question. In such instances the primary concern ought to be the best possible course of action for the good of all concerned, which good includes — to be sure — the religious institute, the member himself or herself, the diocese in question and, above all, the genuine needs of the people of God who are to be served.

Elizabeth McDonough, O.P.

This article originally appeared in *Bulletin on Issues of Religious Law*, Vol. 5, 1989.

16.
ASSOCIATE MEMBERSHIP IN RELIGIOUS INSTITUTES

INTRODUCTION

It is the common estimation within canonical circles that the period of experimentation has now ended with the promulgation of the revised Code of Canon Law. On the other hand, the nature of religious life continues to be an ever-changing dynamic reality. Whether or not these on-going changes are to be considered as "experiments" or as adaptations of religious life, there comes a time when the lived reality must come under canonical review. The aim of law is to order the means to the end in the most appropriate manner. Such is the goal of this paper.

The topic of associate membership is not new, but one that was thought to be covered adequately in the canons and in the living tradition of many religious institutes. In the parlance of the 1917 Code of Canon Law, associate membership was spoken of in terms of membership as a "third order secular," to indicate its lay character, as opposed to "third order regulars," those who professed the three vows in a canonical institute. These lay members were known as tertiaries.

To use the example of the Dominican Order, it has been a long-standing tradition to invite lay men and women to join forces in the spirit and charism of St. Dominic. Local chapters of laity were organized with lay "superiors." Novice directors would see to the instruction of future members. The professions or promises made at that time were truly ceremonial events presided over by both diocesan as well as Dominican priest chaplains.

Since the 1960s, however, the concept of membership by rank — "first order"; "second order"; and "third order" — has been supplanted by the concept of the "Dominican family." The laity are called simply "Dominican laity." (This does not adequately cover the presence of diocesan priests and permanent deacons in their ranks, but they are apparently satisfied with the broader term.) Their participation goes beyond the spirit, theology, and devotions of the Dominican order. They actively join in the apostolic work of Dominican women and men while retaining their status as members of the laity.

In recent years, the general chapters of the Dominican men have raised once more the incorporation of truly dedicated men who have talents to share with their religious brothers. They are spoken of as *donati*, those who identify with the Friars in such a way that they are willing to live the life, donate their talents, and even eventually consider incorporation.

Needless to add, what began centuries ago has blossomed in an ever-increasing participation by the laity in the works and charism of religious institutes.

I. Canonical Definitions

The terms of the 1917 Code used to describe such relationships were found in canon 702. Members formed third orders, pious associations, or confraternities. As Bouscaren explains in his commentary on the 1917 Code, members of the third order seculars had a true rule, could wear the habit of the institute, participated in a novitiate, and did profess private vows. He also notes, under canon 704, §1, that one who has taken vows in a religious institute could not at the same time belong to a secular third order.

The 1983 Code describes associate membership in canon 303 only in terms of a third order relationship. Their participation includes such factors as leading an apostolic life, striving for perfection, and sharing the spirit of a particular religious community, while at the same time living in the world. The distinguishing element of the third order secular from regular continues to be the profession of the three vows in a religious institute with all the rights and obligations of the institute.

II. Present Developments

In the years following Vatican II, however, a tremendous change has taken place in the understanding of lay associates or volunteers.

Originally written for *LCWR Occasional Papers*, October 1989, "The Associate Movement in Religious Life," by Rose Marie Jasinki, C.B.S. and Peter C. Foley, also appeared in *Review for Religious*. It recounts a 1989 meeting of more than a hundred directors of religious associate memberships who gathered to share the histories of their associate movements.

In summary, the authors give us the following points for consideration:

> 1. Who are these associate members? They are women and men, single and married, people of differing faiths, some clergy and religious of other congregations.
>
> 2. What are the reasons motivating them to seek associate membership? The need to:
>   a. Develop a sense of community;
>   b. Deepen prayer life;
>   c. Play a significant role in the community;
>   d. Participate in decision-making, committee functions, chapter meetings.
>
> 3. What has been the evolution of the associate movement?
>   a. 1st generation: those with a desire to be enriched spiritually;
>   b. 2nd generation: those who felt spiritual bonds by reason of having journeyed together as equals;
>   c. 3rd generation: associates active in community life itself;

d. 4th generation: those motivated and supported by a faith community to go out in mission to share the charism.
4. The sense of their commitment: not clear as yet, more "ambiguous."
5. What constitutes a healthy associate program?
   a. A healthy program does not seem to be dependent upon a strong formation program, the type of leadership given by the community, nor the monitoring of associate behavior.
   b. Rather it is dependent upon the quality of relationship between the individual lay person and the religious.
6. What do we see as the directions for the future?
   a. Associate members will not be from the laity alone, but from the union of laity and religious (even from other communities).
   b. Their own conclusion: "The more the congregation included its associates in governance and community structures, the greater the commitment of time and energy of the associates to the religious group."

At this point I wish to thank the members of the School Sisters of St. Francis of Milwaukee, Wisconsin, for the results of a survey conducted in March of 1990 on the question of having associates. Since the documents are lengthy, allow me to quote what the SSSF community sees as the goals for the "Associate Relationship" in ranked order:

1. To provide a structure for mutual relationships between vowed members and associates (81%);

2. To offer support to laity whatever their work or ministry (79%);

3. To provide the option for persons who do not want to make a permanent commitment to religious life (57%);

4. To encourage interest in religious life (57%);

5. To give shape to a new form of religious life (57%);

6. To provide organization for people who want to support SSSF (52%).

One other interesting fact concerns participation of the associates in governmental structures. The report indicates that two-thirds of the community respondents to the survey support the associates being active members of area communities. But the report also adds that what "active" means is less clear.

III. Canonical Considerations

In an article entitled "Lay Associate Programs; Some Canonical and Practical Considerations," David F. O'Connor, S.T., gives us a thorough set of conclusions and cautions concerning the question. These can be summarized as follows:

1. It is more accurate not to refer to these associates or affiliates as members since their involvement is for a limited time period and their commitment has varying degrees.

2. A commitment to celibate chastity in an ecclesial institute demands an appropriate common life and community lifestyle.

3. Some adaptation and accommodation can be made so that the work of evangelization can be aided by the cooperation of lay women and men who are prepared to live and serve with the community on a temporary basis.

4. In making such adjustments, certain values must be maintained in a balanced way: the demands of a community life for those with a celibate commitment; the demands of the apostolate; the need to integrate lay members in a truly cooperative venture.

5. Practical planning is necessary to utilize the true skills of the laity in a way that respects their own distinctive vocations.

6. The program calls for clear goals and expectations and is best achieved through written agreements regarding responsibilities and expectations.

7. The volunteer and lay missioner program is not a vocation effort to foster new recruits for the religious life even if this does occur.

8. While not "members" of the institute in the full sense, lay volunteers and associates do function significantly at the local level. Hence, these members need to be brought into decision-making in matters that affect their daily life and apostolate.

9. Not every one who applies is necessarily suited for this type of cooperative venture. Careful selection and preparation of all involved will allow the personnel to complement one another.

10. As with any other program, periodic evaluation of the program and the personnel is a necessary component if the program is to succeed.

IV. Assessing the Present Situation

Having cited O'Connor's conclusions, I note a tendency to say that any and all questions have been answered. But this seems not to be the case. With so much more being written on the subject and so much more taking place at the grassroots level, the question that comes to mind, first of all, is whether O'Connor's observations still hold true. Given the development in the last five years, what canonical position should be enunciated?

My own first priority is to make a distinction between the life of the institute per se and the external expression of that life as manifested in the apostolate. This distinction does not mean that the life of a consecrated religious is so divided that one element does not enter into and permeate the other. We have only to read canon 673 to learn that "the apostolate of all religious consists primarily in the witness of their consecrated life, which they are bound to foster through prayer and penance." Living the vowed life is an apostolate.

My reason for introducing this element in the discussion is to point out that one who engages in a specific apostolate does not necessarily have to embrace the totality of that institute's commitment. One does not have to be in vows to join in the mission of a community. However, in reading and listening to the discussions on the subject, one begins to pick up the definite desire to have apostolic volunteers become "members." Repeating what I previously mentioned, but in contrast, I pose the question: Does exercising an apostolate mean one should live the vowed life?

I therefore agree with O'Connor's initial observation, i.e., it is not appropriate to use the terminology of membership to designate those women and men who collaborate with us in our ministries. It may very well be inspired by the sincere hope of stimulating our lay colleagues to give serious consideration to a lifetime commitment in religious life. But insofar as we are discussing lay participation in the apostolic endeavors of religious institutes, it is misleading to use the terminology of membership.

This argument is open to further distinction. Some may counter that the word member is being used in an analogous sense and that full identity with the community was never intended. Furthermore, in reading O'Connor's conclusions, we read his statement: "In some real way, the lay associates are 'members' at the local level even though they are not members of the institute." In addition, he makes a strong recommendation that lay associates participate at the local level in decision-making that affects the use of their talents. Otherwise, as he points out, the efforts to coordinate ministries will end in frustration and disillusionment. I can agree with his conclusions but with the notation that the membership referred to remains one of coordinating apostolic endeavors.

What is at stake in my argument is the maintenance and protection of the elements that constitute the vowed life. The canons on institutes of consecrated life are clear in what the institute promises a candidate upon completion of the novitiate and profession of vows.

ADMISSION TO MEMBERSHIP PROMISES:

1. The right to live together in community (cc. 602; 665);

2. The observance of the three vows (cc. 598-601; 666; 668);

3. An interior and exterior prayer life nourished by the sacraments (cc. 663-664);

4. The means to live out the charism and spirit of the founder or foundress (c. 670);

5. Following upon the witness of the vowed life is the possibility of engaging in apostolates in accord with the nature of the community (cc. 673-677).

The attempts to blend together full membership and associate membership have led to confusion in some aspects of the life. I would point out, first of all, the area of government. Upon the establishment of an institute, one of the immediate consequences is the institute's rights to govern itself in accordance with common and proper law (cc. 586-587; 596; 662).

Decision-making in the last three decades since Vatican II has happily embraced the components of dialogue, shared responsibility, collegiality, and subsidiarity. We have moved from unilateral law-making to norms arrived at collegially. The norms that govern our lives remain the prerogative of its members. Introducing delegates at assemblies and chapters from outside the community but with shared rights is not in the best interest of the religious community. There are, however, constitutions and directories that do so. Also, we read in the SSSF report of the strong desire to have associates participate in selection of area leadership.

A second element that is alluded to in the discussion on membership is the whole gamut of formation issues. Membership is achieved through carefully elaborated stages beginning with the evaluation and acceptance of a candidate, the novitiate experience, and finally the days of temporary profession. If the associate membership remains one of apostolic collaboration, then formation is less of an issue. However, if the associate enters into the community's interior life, more care has to be exercised. As O'Connor notes:

> Many of the day-to-day issues of community life: sharing the same building, coming to a common table, adjusting to the variety of personalities, etc., can become unnecessarily tension-filled ... unless the basic ground rules have been agreed upon by all from the beginning. A healthy and welcoming Christian environment can be created only if people know who they are and what roles and expectations they have to meet.

Lastly, the strong mandate to evaluate an associate program brings with it a whole host of practical issues that were scarcely thought of in a previous era. The relationship between the institute and its associate program calls for a contractual agreement. It is at this point that the material of the three vows comes to mind.

Certainly the commitment to consecrated chastity has to take a primary place in any negotiations for shared life and/or ministry. It is the prerogative of each community to state its own goals in this area as religious open up their communities to their lay associates.

But even more crucial in the present setting is the mutually agreed upon norms for setting up the financial arrangements. What financial remuneration will be extended to the associate? How will health insurance, retirement benefits, etc., be covered? What expenses are presumed to belong to the individual and not to the community, e.g., car maintenance, car insurance, vacation time, sick leave, etc.? Some very stressful situations have occurred because of the failure to foresee the possibility of serious health problems that can drain a community's resources. In one instance, after the community had agreed to cover medical insurance, the associate suffered a heart attack which necessitated a heart bypass operation. The outcome was the doctor's verdict that the individual could no longer be employed. Who was to pay for the retirement?

The vow of obedience affects all in every form of religious life. There are people in leadership positions who set the direction in religious life and its service to God's people. There is a chain of command, persons who come to office through the established norms of common and proper law. The associate program will have to incorporate such a chain of command.

Inevitably, the question of evaluation leads to the possible termination of an individual from the program. We have accepted the fact in religious life that some vocations are temporary. Likewise, an associate may make only a temporary commitment and the institute may itself determine that the associate should not continue. While the dedication in ministry may be unqualified, the time lines need to be drawn for the good of the individual and the good of the community.

V. Looking to the Future

In the process of evolution, new forms come into being. As religious and their lay associates share their vocations and their call to witness to God's love for his Church, something new is emerging. The immediate thought that comes to mind is the brief statement of canon 605:

> The approval of new forms of consecrated life is reserved to the Apostolic See. Diocesan Bishops, however, are to endeavor to discern new gifts of consecrated life which the Holy See entrusts to the Church. They are also to assist promoters to express their purposes in the best possible way, and to protect these purposes with suitable statutes, especially by the application of the general norms contained in this part of the code.

The machinery already exists for the establishment of new forms of consecrated life, societies of apostolic life, and secular institutes. This canon looks to the future and lays the groundwork for other possibilities of answering the call to live religious life. It might very well be that the "generations" spoken of in the article quoted above will lead to some formal recognition.

What is to prevent this from coming to pass? In speaking with knowledgeable canonists, they point out the last phrase in the canon: "by the application of the general norms contained in this part of the code." We find ourselves bound by existing canons that characterize religious institutes according to strict norms. What does the future hold? Quite possibly what we need are new canons or directives that recognize the very phenomenon that is taking place among religious institutes and their associates. Experience is the best teacher.

David M. Hynous, O.P.

This article originally appeared in *Bulletin on Issues of Religious Law*, Vol. 6, 1990.

17.
CANON 702, §2 — EQUITY AND CHARITY TO SEPARATED MEMBERS

INTRODUCTION

Thousands of priests, brothers and sisters have departed religious institutes in the years since the close of Vatican Council II. Scholars in various disciplines have reflected on and written about this phenomenon. Administrators of religious institutes and other persons assisting departing religious have been concerned for their welfare and have raised significant questions regarding justice and charity at the time of separation. For many such religious, particularly those who have invested thirty or more years in religious life, separation from a religious institute means traumatic adjustment to a new lifestyle without the support of family and/or friends, or the security of job offers, social contacts and financial resources.

The concerns of major superiors for their departing members prompted a seminar on canon 702, §2 at the October, 1990 annual convention of the Canon Law Society of America in Cleveland, Ohio. The following is a summation of a fourteen-page paper presented at the convention on canon 702, §2 — the equity and charity to separated members. This abbreviated article will follow the basic outline of the paper: 1) a review of the canonical principle underlying religious life; 2) the provision in church law for members departing; 3) the practice of some two hundred seventy-nine religious institutes in the United States regarding separated members. Hopefully, the paper will be helpful in assisting those concerned about departing members and in encouraging more study and planning in this delicate area.

I. THE PRINCIPLE

Before considering canon 702, §2 it is important to review the principle contained in the first paragraph of the same canon which reads:

> Canon 702, §1 — Those who have legitimately left a religious institute or have been legitimately dismissed from one can request nothing from it for any work done in it.

The norm repeats canon 643, §1 of the 1917 Code and reflects the practical effects of religious profession, a total self-donation to the Lord and a promise of service to his people. This traditional teaching of the Church on religious life is contained in *Lumen gentium* 44, and restated in canon 607, §1 of the 1983 Code:

> Canon 607, §1 — Religious life, as a consecration of the whole person, manifests in the Church a wonderful marriage brought about by God, a

sign of the future age. Thus religious bring to perfection their full gift as a sacrifice offered to God by which their whole existence becomes a continuous worship of God in love.

Religious profession is an act of supreme generosity and an absolute and integral renunciation of one's life. The religious places himself or herself in a state of trust and uncertainty with regard to the future. The recompense that a religious receives for work is acquired for the institute, and the institute promises to assume the obligation of supplying what is necessary according to the proper law for achieving the purpose of the member's vocation (c. 661).

It must be remembered that we are not concerned with the personal goods owned before profession or inherited before or after profession by the member. These are dealt with according to canon 668, §§1, 4 & 5 of canon law and the proper law of the institute. Rather, we are considering what the member gains as a member of the institute as stated in paragraph 3 of the same canon:

> Canon 668, §3 — Whatever a religious acquires through personal work or by reason of the institute is acquired for the institute. Unless it is otherwise stated in proper law those things which accrue to a religious by way of pension, subsidy or insurance in any way whatever are acquired for the institute.

II. The Provision

The provision in church law is found in paragraph two of canon 702:

> Canon 702, §2 — The institute however is to observe equity and evangelical charity toward the member who is separated from it.

Canon 643, §2 of the 1917 Code contained the same provision, but it was for women religious. The religious institute was to provide for the safe and becoming return home and enable the woman to live suitably for a specific period of time. Later, this provision was applied to men religious. It is easy to understand the consideration for women at that time, given their dependent and subordinate position in society and the Church.

Since the norms in both the 1917 and 1983 Codes refer to charity and equity, it is well to recall the meaning of equity in canon law.

Equity served as a benign interpretation of Roman law. It corrected the rigidity of the positive law and asserted the claims of natural law. It offered a more balanced solution in harmonizing moral and legal values. Classical canonists believed that mercy and justice meet, and equity tempered the rigor of positive law. Mercy was viewed as a function of justice and wedded to Roman law justice.

Amleto Cardinal Cicognani quoted St. John Chrysostom in his address to the canonists at the 1958 convention of the Canon Law Society of America: "Justice without mercy is not justice, but cruelty, just as mercy without justice is foolishness." After enumerating the many norms in which equity was employed in the 1917 Code,

Cardinal Cicognani exhorted the canonists to employ to the fullest extent canonical equity in the care of souls.

In his address on "Canonical Equity," Pope Paul VI recalled the directive of "wise equity" issued by the first synod of bishops for the revision of church law. Pope Paul VI reminds us that the juridical aspect of the Church has no other end in view than the manifestation of the life of the Spirit — that is, the divine life of the faithful and especially in the matter of charity. He recognizes equity as a higher kind of justice in view of a spiritual end. It softens the rigor of the law and is the fruit of kindness and charity. It takes into account the human person, the exigencies of the situation, and leads to the administering of the law in a more human and understanding manner.

In 1974, the Congregation for Institutes of Consecrated Life and Societies of Apostolic Life (then SCRIS), aware of the great number of departures from religious life, issued a text in the form of a decree. The text, which provided guidelines for major superiors in dealing with members separating, was sent to Father Arrupe, S.J., president of the Union of Superiors General.

The religious institute is obliged to provide for the spiritual, moral, social and temporal welfare of its own members as long as they remain in the institute. To a certain degree, but under a different title and within limits, this obligation was to be extended to those who departed religious life. This assistance would be especially applicable to one who spent a significant period of time in religious life and gave dedicated service to the institute and the Church.

This duty is based on the principles of charity, equity, justice and social responsibility. The major superiors were reminded that conditions today make transition to secular life most difficult, and this adjustment frequently affects the total personality of the one leaving. It is important that such a person know that he or she is treated with respect in accord with human dignity by his or her religious family.

While the decree admitted the impossibility of providing universal norms applicable to all, it offered the following general norms which can be placed under three headings:

1. Need of the Individual — Consideration should be given the education and diplomas received while in the institute, professional experience, and the assurance of a job at departure. Greater solicitude was to be given those members departing with little formal education, advanced in years, in poor health or with limitations which precluded gainful employment.

2. Financial Condition of the Institute — The institute was to give according to its means and in consideration of its obligations to those persevering in religious life.

3. Provisions in Society — Institutes are encouraged to explore and employ present day benefits in society, e.g., social security. Religious institutes are likewise encouraged to establish offices in order to render moral and economic help to those who have left, providing them with counsel in order that they may join the work force and provide suitable employment for themselves.

Religious superiors should interest themselves in the spiritual, social and temporal welfare of those separated from the institute. They should assist departing members during the adjustment period in fitting themselves into society. It is of grave concern to see a religious who has labored many years in a religious institute destitute and unable to provide for basic needs after departure. This is a particular problem in mission countries where monetary provision or social subsidy from the government does not exist. Institutes should study ways to deal with these problems without creating a strict right in justice which would allow the exacting of sums and obligations too burdensome for the institute.

In case of negligence or willing neglect on the part of the religious institute, the departing member can have recourse to the competent diocesan bishop or the Congregation for Institutes of Consecrated Life and Societies of Apostolic Life.

III. The Practice

In March 1990, a questionnaire was distributed by the vicars for religious to the major superiors of religious institutes in their respective dioceses/archdioceses. By mid-June, two hundred seventy-nine institutes responded. Of the sixty-five male religious institutes responding, fifty-three were clerical institutes and twelve were institutes of brothers. One hundred ninety-six apostolic women religious institutes and eighteen monasteries of cloistered women religious responded. The replies to the questionnaire are reproduced on the chart at the end of this article.

In addition to the information supplied, the responses reflected a sincere sensitivity and compassion for the dignity and plight of the individual departing. Several replies from apostolic institutes of women religious encouraged a well-thought-out process during the discernment process. The program consisted of prayer, dialogue, reflection, spiritual direction and counseling. There was evidence of great concern for a departing member who had spent a number of years in the institute and given significant service to the institute and Church.

Consideration was given in many instances to the health, education, potential for employment, and patrimony of the individual. A few institutes took into consideration the salaried individual who would retain the position after departing vis-a-vis one who was stipended and would lose the position. Frequently, the bursar at the general or provincial level assisted the individual regarding financial planning and budgeting.

In some instances, charitable subsidies were given according to the years of service in the religious institute. In most instances health benefits were continued during the period of exclaustration or until the member received employment which provided these benefits. Health benefits had a definite cut-off in almost all of the religious institutes.

Some separated members were given modified benefits or pensions from the retirement plan of the institute. The thinking was that this individual received his or her social security benefit independent of the institute, whereas the social security benefit of the members was given over to the institute.

A few congregations noted that they kept separated members on their mailing lists and would welcome them into the associate program of the institute after a stated period of time.

Conclusion

The response and interest of these two hundred seventy-nine religious institutes in the midst of today's grave financial problems is testimony to their gospel compassion and concern for separating members. A few responders wrote notes expressing gratitude that the issue was being addressed and asked if they could receive the results of the questionnaire. This initial attempt, hopefully, will prompt more study of the issue.

Finally, the study and practice regarding canon 702, §2 raises the following questions:

1. The responses, for the most part, addressed the monetary assistance given departing members. What kind of spiritual and social support should be accorded them?

2. What can be done for nuns leaving cloistered monasteries in mid-life with little formal education and few skills for the job market?

3. Would the Office of Legal Services of the LCWR/CMCM/NATRI consider a study of pension plans for religious institutes that cover, perhaps in a more limited way, those who have separated?

Rose McDermott, S.S.J.

Assistance Given by Religious Institutes To Members At Departure	Men Religious Pontifical 12 Brother Inst. 53 Cleric Inst.	Women Religious Apostolic 163 Pontifical 33 Diocesan	Contemplative Monasteries 17 Pontifical 1 Diocesan
Health Benefits	Yes — 45 (Most indicated a cut-off time.) No — 15 Self-insure — 2 Varies — 3	Yes — 155 (For circumscribed period of time.) No — 41	Yes — 15 (For circumscribed period of time.)
Social Security	Yes — 46 (71%) No — 19 (29%)	Yes — 177 (90%) No — 19 (10%)	Yes — 10 (56%) No — 8 (44%)
Money			
0 – 1,000	5	24	6
1 – 5,000	14	67	4
5 – 10,000	9	12	1
10 – 15,000	3		
15 – 20,000	2	1	
20 – 25,000	1	2	
Need	30	82	14
Varies # Years In	6	11	
Returned Dowry			1

Other Assistance			
Acc. to Need	26	86	6
Car	19	57	3
Used Car or Loan	2	9	
Sold Used Car		5	
None	8		
Retirement Ben.	4	11	
Loan	18	83	3
No Loan	1		
Tuition	1		
Education Help		7	1
Account	1	3	
Apartment Help	1	24	4
Employment Help			2
Furnishings		15	
Clothing		13	3
Counseling		12	1
Inheritance Rtnd			1
Other	2		

This article originally appeared in *Bulletin on Issues of Religious Law*, Vol. 6, 1990.

18.
Recent Developments In Consecrated Life

From earliest times there have been men and women who aspire to follow Christ and imitate His life through the practice of the evangelical counsels. The Church treasures these promptings of the Holy Spirit, and encourages all of her members to foster this form of life that contributes immeasurably to her life and holiness. Competent ecclesiastical authority interprets and regulates the practice of the evangelical counsels, approves the proposals of founders and foundresses, and promotes the many expressions of consecrated life present in the Church.

This esteem of the Church for life consecrated by the profession of the evangelical counsels has been reaffirmed in conciliar teachings and reflected in the 1983 Code of Canon Law. The code includes secular institutes approved in 1947, religious institutes, and societies of apostolic life. The eremitic or anchoritic life, lived within an approved plan of life under the direction of the diocesan bishop, and the life of consecrated virginity, committed to the holy plan of following Christ more closely in dedicated service to the Church, are also recognized forms of consecrated life. While the approbation of new forms of consecrated life is reserved to the Apostolic See, diocesan bishops are directed to discern these new gifts of the Holy Spirit, and to encourage their promoters to express their proposals in suitable norms guided by the general norms of the universal law on consecrated life.

The search of persons for perduring values in today's world, conciliar teaching on the universal call to holiness, and the renewal and adaptation in traditional institutes of consecrated life have contributed significantly to the recent developments in life consecrated by the evangelical counsels. Bishops, vicars for religious, chancellors, and other appropriate diocesan officials are experiencing these stirrings in their respective dioceses. Significant periods of time were expended at the national and regional meetings of the National Conference of Vicars for Religious (NCVR) in addressing issues regarding groups in various dioceses aspiring to become religious institutes. In 1985, a committee of the NCVR drew up guidelines to assist its membership and other diocesan personnel in dealing with this phenomenon in the Church.

In March 1993, a questionnaire was sent to all dioceses in the United States in an attempt to gather some information and insights regarding such recent developments in life consecrated by the evangelical counsels. One hundred one dioceses responded to the questionnaire. Of these, thirty-nine dioceses had no new developments. Sixty-two dioceses reported various developments and submitted information on the same.

This paper will report the statistical information gathered from the responses to the questionnaire. Following the statistical report, some considerations based on the materials and observations of the respondents will be offered in the hopes of assisting those encountering and monitoring such developments.

It should be noted that many of the developments reported in the various dioceses are in embryonic or initial stages. Because of this, it is understandable that many questions were left unanswered. Perhaps these same developments can be revisited in the not too distant future in order to study the progressive development and contribution of these individuals and groups to the life and mission of the Church.

I. Eremitic/Anchoritic Life — Canon 603

Approximately twenty-nine dioceses reported the presence of hermits or candidates, both men and women, for the eremitic lifestyle. Fourteen hermits have made vows in the hands of their diocesan bishops and presented to the same bishop a lifestyle of prayer, penance, and solitude for his approval. Seven candidates are being formed in the eremitical lifestyle in various dioceses.

Six groups — composed of eight, four, three (three groups), and two hermits — live together or in larvae-like structures in five dioceses. The groups are composed of either men or women, or both men and women. Each group has been brought together by a person who experienced the call to have a community of persons living the anchoritic life of prayer, penance, and solitude in a diocese. One diocesan priest lives the life of a hermit with a well-delineated plan for a community. At the time of the questionnaire, he had no followers.

Two religious institutes have permitted two of their members in perpetual profession to live the eremitical life together, and one institute sponsors one of its members that lives this lifestyle. A third religious institute is sponsoring a house of prayer wherein a group of anchorites live under the auspices of a qualified member of the institute. One monastery sponsors an associate who lives the eremitical lifestyle and is under the direction of a monk belonging to the monastic community.

It should be noted here that these latter experiments would not come under canon 603, since they are accountable to the competent authority of the religious institute that sponsors them. In such instances, those living the eremitical life are either members of the religious institute in perpetual profession, subject to the rule or constitutions and superiors of the institute, or individuals affiliated with or sponsored by the institute and under its auspices.

II. Order of Virgins — Canon 604

Twenty-two dioceses reported the presence of consecrated virgins and candidates being formed for the order of virgins. The responses to the questionnaire indicate that there are twenty-three women who have received the rite and who belong to the order of virgins in their particular dioceses. One diocese has four women belonging to the order of virgins; five have two women, and nine dioceses each have one consecrated virgin.

Fifteen women are preparing to be admitted to the order of virgins through a formation process monitored by a member of the diocesan curia. While a few dioceses reported more than one consecrated virgin and/or candidate for the order of virgins, no response indicated that there was an association of these consecrated virgins in the diocese in accord with canon 604, §2. This may be because only one diocese had four consecrated virgins at the time of the questionnaire.

III. Institutes of Consecrated Life

A. Religious Institutes — Canon 607

Twenty-three dioceses reported groups that were aspiring to become diocesan religious institutes. A religious institute is a society in which the members pronounce public vows, either perpetual or temporary according to the proper law, and live a life in common as brothers or sisters. One diocese reported six such groups, five dioceses reported three groups, and three dioceses reported two groups. The remaining fourteen dioceses each had one group of persons aspiring to become a religious institute.

Of these forty-one groups, one had been approved as a religious institute of diocesan right at the time of the questionnaire. This was a group of twenty-four women religious who had separated themselves from their former institute of pontifical right. Another group of six men had been approved as a *sui iuris* priory of diocesan right. The other groups were in various stages of development. Thirty-six were private associations of the faithful, and five were public associations of the faithful with approved statutes. The latter seemed to have more members and greater stability.

Some responses did not give the number of persons in these groups aspiring to become diocesan religious institutes. However, the numbers reported were very low. Only one group had eighteen persons, two had ten, one had nine, and two had eight members. The other groups had significantly lower numbers, some with but two persons as members. A few of the groups were affiliated with a traditional religious institute of either pontifical or diocesan right, while attempting to become a diocesan institute.

B. Secular Institutes — Canons 710-712

Two dioceses reported groups that aspire to become secular institutes. This is an institute of consecrated life in which the members live in the world, assume the practice of the evangelical counsels according to the constitution of the institute, and exercise their consecration in apostolic activity. Each of these two groups has the status of a public association, one having five members, the other, three members.

C. Societies of Apostolic Life — Canon 731

Four dioceses reported fledgling groups aspiring to the status of societies of apostolic life. These institutes are comparable to institutes of consecrated life. The members live as brothers or sisters in common while pursuing the apostolic purpose of the society in accord with their constitutions. In some societies of apostolic life, the members embrace the evangelical counsels according to the constitutions; in others, they strive for the perfection of charity through the observance of the constitutions. Two of these groups have but five and two members. The third has been in existence since 1979, with no additional members. The fourth has a membership of two hundred living in that particular diocese and elsewhere. It is composed of priests, women religious, and laity affiliated with the group of priests. The report on this group seemed somewhat to reflect the traditional first, second, and third orders.

IV. New Forms — Canon 605

Two groups composed of clerics, vowed men and women, and laity were reported as desiring to become new forms of consecrated life. One group had thirty-four members in one diocese, while the other claimed seventy-seven in various parts of the United States and elsewhere. Both are presently private associations. In reading the reports on these new forms of consecrated life, it was difficult to determine precisely the qualities that distinguish them from the already approved forms of consecrated life in the Church.

V. Non-canonical Groups

Twenty-six dioceses reported the presence of non-canonical groups in their midst. For the most part, these were very small groups of two, three, four, or five members. It would seem from reading the explanations of the respondents that either the group did not approach the bishop or a diocesan official to petition for canonical status, or they were advised that they needed to present an account of their lifestyle and attract more members before any serious discussion regarding their status could be entertained by the diocesan bishop. In a few instances, the groups made it known that they did not wish to petition for canonical status.

The Sisters for Christian Community were reported in sixteen dioceses numbering approximately sixty-five, with twelve being the highest concentration in a given diocese. Eight Brothers for Christian Community were reported in various dioceses, with three being the highest concentration in a given diocese.

VI. Observations

These persons and groups of persons are still in the beginning stages in the particular forms of consecrated life. Therefore, it is premature at this time to study in depth their particular gift or charism, or to evaluate their contribution to the life and mission of the Church. However, it would seem that wise planning on the part of diocesan bishops or officials delegated by the diocesan bishop to assist these individuals and groups may be invaluable to them in the present during the formative process, and in the future in avoiding serious problems and enabling stability. The responses to the questionnaire and the observations of some respondents raise the following concerns in the areas of diocesan monitoring and policies.

A. EREMITICAL LIFE AND CONSECRATED VIRGINITY

1. ADMISSION AND FORMATION

The eremitical/anchoritic life and the life of consecrated virginity find their roots in the first centuries of the Church. Gradually, these lifestyles were lived out within the constructs of religious orders for hundreds of years. In the 1983 Code of Canon Law, a hermit can publicly profess the evangelical counsels in the hands of the diocesan bishop and observe his or her plan of life under his direction (c. 603). A diocesan bishop can, according to the approved liturgical rite, consecrate virgins committed to the holy plan of following Christ more closely and dedicated to service in the Church (c. 604).

It would seem that the potential for hermits and consecrated virgins within the diocesan community and beyond the parameters of religious institutes places a certain responsibility on the bishops willing to accept these forms of consecrated life in their dioceses. Therefore, it would be well for those delegated by the diocesan bishops to monitor such lifestyles to become knowledgeable regarding their history, and to be familiar with the canonical norms on admission and formation in religious life.

The eremitic life lived in prayer, penance, silence, and solitude — and a life of consecrated virginity lived in an intimate following of Christ and apostolic service, but without communal support — would seem to prompt wise policies around suitable age, and qualities of health, character, and maturity. Appropriate testimonials of baptism, confirmation, and registration in a parish should be gathered before the person is given hope of being admitted as a candidate for the eremitical life or the order of virgins. The impediments for admission to the novitiate in a religious institute should likewise be addressed.

Respondents to the questionnaire observed that many of these men and women seeking an eremitical lifestyle or a life of consecrated virginity have departed religious institutes or societies of apostolic life. It would be well to have some testimony from the competent authority in the respective institute as to the performance of the person during the length of time he or she spent in the institute. Copies of indults of departure from the former institute should be requested by the bishop or his delegate.

Some candidates for these lifestyles have received very fine formation in the former institutes of consecrated life, and the bishops were pleased with the background they brought to the life of a hermit or consecrated virginity. The respondents noted that there were other aspirants to these lifestyles with very little background. They had no formal preparation nor instruction in prayer, Sacred Scripture, liturgy, the theology of the evangelical counsels, the nature of the lifestyle they sought to embrace, nor an intelligent understanding of the Church and its structures.

Both the eremitic way of life and a life of consecrated virginity lived alone without the support of a community would seem to warrant a qualified diocesan director knowledgeable in the lifestyle, and competent to advise the diocesan bishop and to assist the candidates. Likewise, these persons should have spiritual directors and periodic meetings with the diocesan bishop or his vicar for religious. It is noteworthy that some monasteries provided that a monk live a significant number of years in community life before being permitted to live the life of a solitary. Also, for a great period of time, the Church forbade the consecration of virgins outside the parameters of cloistered life, or, in a few instances, institutes of women religious of a monastic tradition with simple vows. From this it would seem that careful preparation, healthy interpersonal relationships, and communal support are recognized as important for these lifestyles. It is interesting to note the provision for the associations of virgins in canon 604, §2.

The bishop or his delegate should seek the wise counsel of the diocesan director and other knowledgeable persons in determining the acceptance and formation of such persons. Likewise, this director can be of assistance as the hermit plans his or her way of life for the approval of the diocesan bishop. In a few instances, the women desiring to be consecrated virgins belonged to a secular third order. They already followed an approved lifestyle of personal and liturgical prayer and dedicated service to the Church. In most instances, however, the candidates to these lifestyles need someone knowledgeable and practical to assist them from the start in making wise decisions and provisions to live out their vocation.

2. Financial Stability

Many respondents to the questionnaire did not indicate how the hermits, anchorites, and consecrated virgins provided for their temporal necessities. Since many of the women admitted to the order of virgins were former religious, they seemed to have sufficient education and skills to acquire positions in the various diocesan or secular structures. But given the highly contemplative nature of the eremitical lifestyle, finances for board, health benefits, and retirement provisions can be most problematic in an increasingly complex society.

This practical issue should be frankly discussed with the candidate both at the time of the interview and during the formative process. A few bishops required candidates for the eremitical lifestyle and the order of consecrated virginity to sign a waiver stating that neither the hermit or consecrated virgin, nor any member of their families, would expect any remuneration or financial assistance from the diocese. Bishops should be careful in admitting persons to these particular forms of consecrated life who may later prove to be a significant liability to the diocese. While in strict justice there may be no obligation to assist such persons, there may well be some demands based on equity and charity.

B. INSTITUTES OF CONSECRATED LIFE

It would seem wise to have carefully delineated diocesan policies in place for those persons wishing to found institutes of consecrated life. Some guidelines are already available from the National Conference of Vicars for Religious (1985), and in the publication of the Canon Law Society of America's *Roman Replies and CLSA Advisory Opinions 1992* (c. 579). The following are a few observations that should be kept in mind during the initial stages of groups aspiring to become diocesan institutes.

1. UNIQUE GIFT OR CHARISM

Many respondents to the questionnaire reported that frequently the potential founder or foundress presented a way of life or spirituality already present and operative in the life of the Church. It would be well from the beginning to advise the person of this fact, and to recommend that he or she consider seeking admission to that particular order or congregation. Many of the persons seeking to found new diocesan institutes were reported to have departed traditional institutes of consecrated life due to disagreements with the renewal and adaptation efforts following the Second Vatican Council. The respondents to the questionnaire noted, and a careful reading of the submitted materials confirmed, that many of the proposals for new institutes of consecrated life or societies of apostolic life frequently repeated traditions of religious life already present in the Church.

2. PERSONAL AND COMMUNAL QUALITIES

The age, qualities, testimonials, and impediments for admission to the novitiate of a religious institute, and the documents and testimonials noted above for the eremitical/anchoritic lifestyle and the life of a consecrated virgin, would apply to the founder/foundresses and their members. Groups aspiring to become institutes of consecrated life should be closely monitored by periodic visits from the vicar for religious or the person designated by the diocesan bishop. These visits would afford opportunities to interview the individuals, to observe the common life of the group, their relationships with one another and the founder or foundress, and their apostolic activities. The visitor should also inquire as to the financial stability of the group.

Likewise, the visit would be an opportunity to encourage the founder or foundress to reflect on his or her inspiration or charism, and to begin to write in draft form the proposed way of life for review by the bishop or his delegate. The vicar for religious or delegate of the diocesan bishop should assist the founder or foundress in formulating these inspirations and plan into a proper law in conformity with the general law of the Church for consecrated life. Observations should be kept in the diocesan file on the group regarding this plan of life, the curriculum vitae of the founder or foundress and the other members, their perseverance or turn-over, the formation and preparation of new members, observations made during visitation regarding common life and apostolic activity, the financial stability of the group, and its assimilation into and acceptance by the broader ecclesial community.

If the group shows good potential for becoming an institute of diocesan right, it would be well for the bishop to inform the Congregation for Institutes of Consecrated Life and Societies of Apostolic Life regarding the nature, purpose and end of the institute, and to give a brief introductory report. This remote preparation is helpful at the time of the formal consultation with the same Congregation in obtaining the *nihil obstat*.

3. Stages and Parameters of Time

Finally, the diocesan policies should place reasonable parameters of time for the group to reflect on its charism, attract members, attain financial security, and promote apostolic activity in keeping with the pastoral plan of the diocese and the mission of the Church. In other words, if, after a significant number of years as a private association, there seems to be no unique contribution of the group, no increase in the number of members, no financial stability — or some other substantial lacunae — it would seem just to point out that the group poses no hope for advancing to the status of a public association and eventual approval as a diocesan institute.

The period as a private association should not be hurried; a group can remain as such for years. During the time as a private association, the stability and growth of the group can be monitored by the vicar for religious or other competent diocesan official. It would seem unwise to move a group to the status of a public association with juridic personality unless it has articulated its proper law, attracted a fair amount of members, and proved financial stability. One of the serious reservations of the respondents and this author was the approval of some groups with very few members as public juridic persons. A rescript from CICLSAL sent in by a respondent to the questionnaire stated that forty members are required before a group is approved as a diocesan institute.

It must be stated that, while a few groups claimed to be new forms of consecrated life, no new form of consecrated life was clearly perceived in any of the materials from the sixty-two dioceses. If a new form of consecrated life evolves that differs significantly from religious institutes, secular institutes or societies of apostolic life, the approval of such a new form of consecrated life is reserved to the Apostolic See (c. 605).

VII. Conclusion

This reporter truly appreciates the time and concern the vicars for religious and other diocesan personnel took to respond to the questionnaire and, in some instances, to offer their observations and concerns regarding these developments in consecrated life. Changes in our society and stirrings in traditional institutes of consecrated life join with these reported developments to alert us to an awareness of a gradual transition in life consecrated by the evangelical counsels. History teaches us that this lifestyle in the Church does not remain static and secure, but evolves and develops to address societal and ecclesial needs. During this time of transition, prayer for wisdom and patience, reflection on life experience, and reverence for the goodness and generosity of human persons will bring us to the humility necessary to assist our bishops in discerning the gifts of the Holy Spirit for the good of the Church.

Rose McDermott, S.S.J.

This article originally appeared in *Bulletin on Issues of Religious Law*, Vol. 9, 1993.

19.
Sponsorship

Introduction

In recent years, religious congregations in the United States have shown a strong preference for use of the term sponsorship to describe the congregation's relationship to its established works or to those for which it maintains a public association.

Numerous articles have pointed out that the idea of sponsorship of an institution is a relatively new use of the term; so, while the term sponsorship is now being used with frequency, we have little track record of its meaning in law, either in the civil law or in church law. The short entry for sponsor in *Black's Law Dictionary* suggests a range of contrasting or even contradictory meanings; church law speaks of a sponsor only in the context of certain sacraments.

The lack of a developed legal understanding for sponsorship has some significance. Well-developed legal terms allow us to express a whole bundle of ideas in a single word.

For example, corporation is a well-developed term in civil law. When one speaks of a corporation a very specific type of entity is understood; moreover, a whole body of law is available to consult about how a corporation is established, how it operates, the rights and duties of those who relate to it, how it is dissolved, etc. Similarly, religious institute is a well-developed concept in canon law, and canon law provides a body of law to consult regarding the major aspects of establishing, conducting the affairs of, even dissolving the religious institute. Well-developed terms allow us to speak with clarity; using them, we can reach understanding with ease and move to action with a measure of confidence.

Use of an underdeveloped legal term is more difficult; it requires us to spell out exactly what we mean when we choose to use that term. No standard understanding of the term is available for reference. Each use is based on a particular set of circumstances and its meaning is limited by the interests and by the foresight of those who give it its definition. Sponsorship is such an underdeveloped legal term.

Although underdeveloped in a legal sense, sponsorship is a term that is rich in connotation, a fact that contributes to its use. To examine the various senses one can make of sponsorship, we might reflect on the common meanings of the term, as well as consider some circumstances in which the term is actually being used today by religious congregations.

Common Meaning

A standard dictionary gives these three meanings for "sponsor":

1. A person or agency that undertakes certain responsibilities in connection with some other person or some group or activity, as in being a proponent, endorser, advisor, underwriter, surety, etc.;

2. A godfather or godmother; person who answers for a child, as at baptism, making the profession of faith and the promises prescribed;

3. A business firm or other agency that alone or with others pays the costs of a radio or television program on which it advertises or promotes something.

As used by religious congregations today, sponsorship connotes these elements of the definition: the assumption of responsibilities for mission and identity, maintaining communion with the spiritual source, and a relationship of benevolence.

I. Responsibilities

The first meaning of sponsor speaks of one who has accepted specific responsibilities with respect to some other entity. The responsibilities could range from agreeing to be a "booster" to its agreement to act as surety. A sponsor could agree to promote the work of an institution by responding to opportunities to join in support of it or to use influence on its behalf, or it could financially back an institution (to act as surety, guaranteeing the debts of the institution with its own funds). Or it could agree to somehow endorse the institution (by associating its name or reputation with it) or to serve as advisor to it or to provide resources for, or to vouch for or provide backing for, the institution or some aspect of it.

Many congregations that use the term sponsorship can show a sponsorship document that has been worked out by the congregational leadership and under which the board of the institution operates, a document that defines or describes the responsibilities of the relationship. The sponsorship can be as broad or as narrow as are the interests and concerns of the religious congregation. Sponsorship documents exist with or without provision for congregational representation in the governing structure of the institution.

Participation in the governing structure (most often through the exercise of reserved powers by a member class) may be necessary if a congregation is concerned either:

— to safeguard the dedication of property or of endowments to a certain use; or

— to safeguard the identity and promote the mission of the institution itself, for example, to operate within a certain religious tradition or to sustain the congregation's close public identification with the institution.

II. Examples

There are cases, however, where participation in governance might not be necessary. If the congregation's interests, and therefore the terms of its sponsorship, are limited to a narrow, well-defined set of concerns and responsibilities, the document might stand alone as an agreement between the congregation and the institution. This is illustrated in the following examples:

Case One

A congregation decides to withdraw from active engagement with a school and settles property matters with a corporation whose lay board wishes continued use of the school name, a name that is long associated with the congregation. An agreement between the lay board and the congregation might allow for continued use of the name under clear conditions: for example, that the school remain publicly identified as Catholic, the diocesan curriculum for religious education be followed, and access be granted to some person or group delegated by the congregation to assure that conditions for use of the name are being met. This congregation's sponsorship relates to a very particular aspect of identity and nothing more.

Case Two

In a further example, a congregation decides to withdraw from operating a hospital and enters into a merger agreement with a larger hospital. Under the agreement the congregation will appoint personnel and the hospital will fund a specific program within the institution for certain children at risk. The agreement sets out all the terms of this limited sponsorship arrangement, conditions for its operation and its termination, including the amount that will be paid to the congregation in compensation should the hospital unilaterally terminate the program and its funding.

In these cases, use of a sponsorship agreement indicates that the sponsoring congregation has determined to formalize its relationship with an institution in specific and limited ways. What had perhaps originated as an activity of the congregation itself — part of the family business — continues autonomously, with a specific, but limited reference to the founding congregation. In these examples, the congregation had once conducted the activity; now it is its sponsor in some limited and publicly agreed upon way. Where previously the operation of the congregation and the institution had been intertwined and hard to distinguish, in this limited new role the congregation's identity is made distinct from the institution's identity. The institution does not speak for the sponsor, nor the sponsor for the institution. The sponsor accepts specific and clearly understood responsibilities and receives the means, information and cooperation needed to carry them out. The agreement is exclusive, that is, it expresses the full understanding of what constitutes the relationship, and nothing that is of interest to the parties, now or for the future, is left unsaid. Any change would require the consent of both congregation and institution.

The two preceding examples illustrate a narrow usage of sponsorship. However, most often the term sponsorship is used with a broader meaning in mind. In these cases, the sponsorship document, if there is one, is not an agreement between parties but a declaration, approved by the congregation, of the philosophy of the institution, its public identity, its purposes, distinguishing characteristics and other such things. The document standing alone has uncertain legal significance. It must be matched with a structure that will insure that each element of the statement holds — both in good times and in bad.

With or without a formal sponsorship document, a congregation exercises sponsorship of an institution typically by a direct governance of the institution through a civil structure or by reserving powers in the civil structure of the institution to a class of members who are the persons charged with administration of the congregation. A reservation of powers to members allows the congregation to exercise vigilance over the identity and the mission of the institution, and any other interest it desires to promote or to safeguard, or to meet the responsibility it has under its own religious law, while at the same time involving lay participation in the institution's governance.

Undertaking specific responsibilities of relationship is at the heart of sponsorship in the first common meaning of the word. The responsibilities require definition and the means to exercise the responsibilities, as well as to receive accountability from all who share responsibility for the mission of the institution.

III. Communion

The second meaning of sponsor carries overtones of the faith tradition, benign regard, non-interference, a spiritual haven in hard times. This spiritual or moral aspect is present in every attempt to describe a sponsorship relationship.

Ultimately it is because the congregation's spirit or charism is important to the identity and to the culture of the institution that the congregation and the institution are in relationship. This is a key aspect of religious sponsorship. Any institution in a faith tradition needs to draw from something deeper than itself to be able to sustain that aspect of its identity through various periods of transition and change. It has need to be in communion with the source of this tradition. Regardless of what else is in place, this aspect of sponsorship requires continual promotion and assent by all who are responsible for the institution and for the congregation.

This spiritual or moral aspect of sponsorship has been worked out in a variety of ways: development of "mission effectiveness" strategies; board, staff or faculty workshops; a hand-book that summarizes or reflects on the spirit of institutions in the congregation's tradition; service programs and liturgies; connection and collaboration with other institutions in the congregation's tradition. All of these are examples of means used to promote the spiritual and moral dimension of sponsored institutions. The very development of these strategies fosters the bonds between congregation and institution.

Thus, in this second sense of sponsorship, the institution connects with something that transcends the particular members associated with it at any one time. For this reason, the congregation itself, as well as individual members of the congregation, are key to mission effectiveness. Relationship with a religious body brings a public recognition, a certain pledge of trustworthiness and a stability and continuity that individuals alone cannot supply, no matter how long-lived or gifted.

IV. BENEVOLENCE

As for the third meaning of sponsor, it suggests the quid pro quo present in a commercial relationship. The sponsor lends support and may, in turn, receive some benefit in terms of good will. The institution receives needed funds or resources and the sponsor enjoys a recognition for making a significant contribution, as well as perhaps some negotiated opportunity to promote its own interests or values. This is the sense in which Mobile Oil sponsors *Mystery Theatre*. Thus, the congregation, as sponsor in this third sense, is essentially a donor, and, as with other donors, the support is freely given and acknowledged. Unless gifts are restricted, they do not obligate.

Religious congregations today have a greater concern for sponsorship issues than perhaps has ever been the case in the past. Changes in the demographics and in the financial obligations of religious congregations, the complexity of operating public institutions today, the concerns of the American Church and the perils of our litigious environment have all played a role. Added to this complex environment are the diverse perspectives, interests and responsibilities of all who are concerned about Catholic institutions: the congregation and its administration, those working in and directing the institution, those who support and benefit from the institution, the local church, members of boards, and others with a role or interest in the institution.

While it is not possible in this article to comment on every aspect of the current and developing sponsorship question, three topics will be given further comment, not because they are, in every case, the most important, but because they often involve issues where congregations may act with unexamined or unwarranted assumptions.

These sponsorship issues involve: identity, liability, and the role of laity in the Church.

V. IDENTITY

Today a great deal is being written and debated on the question of the Catholic identity of institutions that supply valuable secular services — whether they be health services, social services or education. That the Church and religious congregations should continue to play a role in the delivery of these vital human services is apparent to anyone who seriously evaluates the contribution being made by church institutions. They provide valuable human services conferring great benefit on our society. These institutions also are a means to express the concern of Christ and of his Church for all who are in need, and therefore are a necessary part of the mission of the Church in our society.

While the Catholic identity of institutions is a serious question for the whole Church, so too is the question of the identity of religious congregations, their mission and what role the institutions play in that identity.

Because certain works of a religious institute historically have been part and parcel of the very identity of the institute itself, we must be clear and confident about the relationship the congregation maintains to those works, and how the congregation goes about altering those relationships when it is necessary to do so. These works relate to the patrimony of the institute — its nature, purpose, spirit and character. They are often closely linked to the mission of the congregation and the particular gift it brings to the Church.

Religious congregations typically sacrificed the possibility of a segregated provision for the future support of members in order to create and finance institutions that all believed would meet the responsibilities of both mission and support. When it becomes apparent that the economics would fail to meet both responsibilities, separate strategies are needed, often requiring the institutions to become less dependent on contributed services. A reduction of dependence on contributed services (or their equivalent) is a financial decision. The congregation, although less a current donor, is no less responsible for the mission of the institution.

Major decisions regarding works created and developed through the involvement of many members of the congregation over generations would normally require a broad and formal process. To alter the relationship in a fundamental way or to alter the nature of the institution itself affects the very life of the congregation.

The importance of major institutional changes is highlighted in the 1983 Code of Canon Law. Canon 1295 provides that any decision that would jeopardize the patrimonial condition of the institute requires the same approvals as are needed for the sale of the property of the institute.

Thus, questions of the institution's identity and mission are related to the congregation's self-understanding as well as to its public role in the Church. Whether a congregation affirms its relationship to an institution or decides on disassociation, the decision is made in the context of faith in the mission and in the future of the congregation.

If a congregation has no abiding congregational interest in what an institution becomes, it should acknowledge that "up front" and make a decision to move toward alienation of the work, a decision that takes into account every aspect of the situation in which there may be interests to clarify.

However, difficulties arise when a congregation moves to decision about its relationship to an institution, but has not accepted that real consequences will follow such a decision. Before long, the decision made with ambivalence or with too narrow a perspective reveals its weakness. It is a sign of ambivalence, for example, for a congregation to decide both to disengage itself from responsibility for a work and simultaneously to continue to obligate itself in some way for its survival, for example, by accepting unsecured financial arrangements.

A decision to incorporate the work and to operate it as an independent civil entity does not, in and of itself, signal an intention to distance the institution from the mission of the congregation. To initiate a separate incorporation of an activity is often a prudent decision. In fact, canon law requires congregations to use civil means to safeguard property and works for the mission of the Church.

A decision to transfer property has greater significance in cases where there is an independent board for the work and where it is assumed that the property will continue to be available for other congregational purposes, for example, as living space for the members or for some other activity of the congregation. Because property titled in the institutional corporation will be viewed by the board as dedicated solely for the work of the institution, any other use is poorly protected by unwritten understandings and assumptions.

For the same reason that a congregation would not permit community property to be titled in the name of individual members (it is not a question of trust), it is equally imprudent (and unheedful of church law) to disregard the consequences of placing community property or total governance of a community work in the hands of an independent group without making explicit provision for the eventualities of the further changes that will occur. This is true whether the independent group happens to include a number of religious or is all lay.

Equally ambivalent may be a decision to maintain full commitment to an institution while allowing it to network or to consolidate its operations with institutions that are either sponsored by other congregations or are not Catholic.

Membership Model

A typical method of continuing responsibility for a work and involving others in its governance, a common consideration in sponsorship arrangements, is the use of a membership-type governance structure. Acting as corporate members, the persons who are in the congregation's leadership role exercise within the corporation significant responsibilities for safeguarding the identity, mission and property of the corporation for the purposes for which the corporation was established. Under typical state law, the board of directors (or trustees) has all the powers of governing except those explicitly reserved in the documents of the corporation to those described as corporate members. Reserved powers typically include those of appointment and removal of the operational head and of the members of the board and its chair, approval of any essential document, approval of indebtedness and sale of property, and a right to appointment of an independent auditor with receipt of its report.

While the membership model gives freedom to move with new developments that affect the institution, the model is not without difficulty. One example of this occurs where institutions would embark on joint ventures, or otherwise operate in complex or highly specialized situations. If several congregations are involved in establishing a joint venture, how are the on-going concerns of each taken into account, without over-burdening the arrangement or rendering it too unstable?

A further concern raised about the membership model is the opinion that it requires a high level of involvement on the part of the congregation's administration. This concern bears some examination. Corporate members do not, in fact, have an involvement to the degree of board involvement. The members are not responsible for the operations of the institution; the board is. The duties of the members parallel the canonical responsibilities of the council for the congregation, and it is important that they and the members of the congregation do not use the role of member to Monday-morning quarterback the administrator or to micro-manage. The members appoint and they replace; they do not perform any of the roles of the administrator, and they normally are not the principal group to evaluate the administrator. Equally important, however, is that the corporate members do not view their role as a pro forma one (as a rubber stamp); they are the ultimate guardians of the mission of the institution. They must be satisfied that the institution is fulfilling its mission. If dissatisfied, they must replace those whom they have entrusted with this charge.

In some situations of the past, congregations have removed themselves from a governance role because they thought their presence would compromise the well-being of the institutions. A separate incorporation with a self-perpetuating board (that is, a board that elects its own members) became a model used by many colleges. In some parts of the country it had been feared that a structured role for congregational members in the governance of a college would disqualify the college from government funding. This proved an unfounded fear and the highest courts have held it not disqualifying for a religious congregation to have a structured role in the governance of a college.

For the congregation, a separate incorporation or a transfer of its property may in effect be a decision to stabilize property for a particular apostolic purpose. Stabilization is similar to the establishment of a trust. The congregation sets down the purposes of the institution, as well as the events that would either return the property (or its value) to some other entity dedicated to the work of the institute, as the civil law would allow, or would trigger the dissolution of the corporation.

Many eventualities must be foreseen in forging new arrangements of relationship or commitment. A sponsorship arrangement needs to work (that is, be clear, unambiguous and enforceable) in a variety of possible situations, including one that would require replacement of a board or the removal of the chief administrator (whether a member of the congregation or otherwise). Risk-taking should not be confused with imprudence. Every current intention of the congregation must be made explicit and be incorporated into well-drafted documents, and there must be provision for dealing with the unforeseen.

VI. LIABILITY

The specter of litigation has raised the comfort-level of dealing with separate civil structures. Founders of religious houses in the United States formed civil corporations to hold title to property or to receive a license or charter to conduct an activity, but they did not look to separate incorporation of activities for the reasons we do today. In the last century lawsuits for damages did not pose a serious threat to religious congregations. Nearly every state had what were known as charitable immunity laws. This meant that the beneficiary of a charity could not sue the charity for damages resulting from the torts or negligence of its employees. The institution could be sued for other reasons, for example for its contracts and other obligations. The law, however, gave immunity from its greatest danger, liability for negligence and torts. Immunity was a way to protect valuable charitable activity as well as to insure that gifts made to charity would be available for the purposes for which they were given.

Complete charitable immunity exists today in very few places — Arkansas is one. Some states have a limit on the amount certain charities can be sued for — either a fixed amount ($20,000 for hospitals in Massachusetts, for example) or the amount of insurance (as in Maine). Until the last few years the trend had been toward removing protections for charities. Today, there is a trend toward reinstatement of limitations on the liabilities of charities, particularly to protect volunteer activity and to establish caps on beneficiary claims.

While the purchase of insurance is the best means to achieve the protection of assets (periodic review of insurance limits is a must!), in some situations the risk of not purchasing sufficient coverage continues to be a real one. For a congregation that carries on several activities, a separate incorporation of each distinct activity provides a clear demarcation of what is at risk in the operation of each.

Congregations are entitled to the use and to the full protection of laws limiting liabilities, in the same way as businesses and other charities receive these protections.

Consider a family whose members conduct several businesses through several corporations. They do not risk loss of all the assets of the various corporations in a lawsuit against one corporation simply because they, as owners, are related to each other. Corporation assets are also beyond the reach of a claim against a family member for something unrelated to any of the corporate activities. In a similar way, Corporation A can own stock in Corporation B and risk no more than the value of the stock if Corporation B is sued.

The Corporate Veil

The feared "piercing of the corporate veil" means that, under certain circumstances, a corporation will be held responsible for the actions of another corporation or for the actions of the other corporation's employees. The test is whether, in fact, distinct activities are being carried on in these corporations. Is school A in reality a distinct operation from hospital B or school C or from corporation D established to conduct other business of the congregation? It matters not that members of the congregation are involved in all of these or that they are assigned to work in them by the congregation. The question is whether or not from a civil point of view they are a single enterprise. Are the activities conducted and the finances handled in a way that indicates that the institutions and corporations are conducted as distinct activities?

When it comes to liability, the members of a religious institute and the separately incorporated activities of the institute should be viewed civilly in the same way as the family and its business corporations. Religious institutes are often unfairly put to the test of proving that their members are not agents of the congregation at every turn.

A major purpose for forming a corporation is to limit any potential loss to the assets of that corporation — and to prevent recovery against the property of individual persons or against other corporations.

From the viewpoint of the congregation, forming a corporation, and limiting the potential for loss, should not exclude a role for a congregation in guiding the work toward the ends for which it was established. There are numerous ways in which corporations accept control and limitation from outside agencies, without the outside agencies becoming responsible for the corporation or its liabilities.

An incorporated organization can establish a wide range of obligations and relationships. Private industry and hospitals accept enormous controls as the price of doing business with the government and of receiving government money. These controls and standards do not transform the business or hospital into a government agency, and somehow render the government liable for their activities. Schools open their doors to accreditation agencies and supply an enormous amount of information; they accept recommendations and evaluation as a condition for continuing to be recognized as meeting educational standards. State education agencies intervene in significant ways to set standards or to evaluate and even reform when there is cause to question educational results and can dismiss and replace a board when necessary. The state education departments and the accrediting agencies are not held responsible for the acts of the institution.

The leadership of a congregation must see with two sets of eyes. As the governing group of a religious congregation, it acts under its constitutions for the congregation, to carry out its distinctive mission for the Church. However, the civil law in the United States does not recognize the acts of a religious institute, as does the civil law in some countries. We need to be clear, therefore, that civil acts and civil structures are needed to effect and to protect the whole of the purposes for which corporations were established. Without substituting civil government for religious government, or without confusing the two, issues of religious life and issues of civil law must be addressed each in its own sphere.

VII. Role of the Laity

In the spirit of Vatican Council II, religious have been challenged to exercise their apostolates with a greater sense of collaboration, including collaboration with lay colleagues. The lay person and the religious each bring personal gifts and the gifts of their Christian dedication to the work. Individually, the religious has no justification to view the work as more his or her work than it is the institution's work of his or her lay colleague. This new-found understanding of the commitment of lay Catholics is a welcome development.

But some go further and urge religious congregations to turn over their works to members of the laity and to share governance with the laity, as if this, too, were an injunction of Vatican Council II. To whom or to what are the congregations being asked to deliver their patrimony?

While the law of the Church provides for recognition of lay associations formed within the Church for the apostolate, each lay person, like each individual religious, has status only as an individual person in the Church.

We know that some religious do not see with clarity the difference between themselves as individuals and the congregations to which they belong. Some religious talk about themselves as tax exempt (when only organizations have tax exempt status). Or some few religious see no problem in living an independent religious life, as if being a religious is a quality of the person.

The greater majority of religious see their congregations as a reality into which they have entered and as a living tradition they will hand on to some generations to come. In that spirit, they are guardians and promoters of the charism of the congregation, custodians of its works and trustees for the future. The "laity" involved in the governance of Catholic institutions are persons who carry no particular responsibility for the charism or the mission of a congregation and sometimes have no ties to the Church. Should the survival of institutions be more important than the public witness for which they were founded?

In the February 18, 1994 issue of the *National Catholic Reporter*, Joan Chittister raises the challenge of the relationship of religious life to ministry:

> [R]eligious must ask themselves what they stand for as communities and who knows it. When we stood for education and health services and the care of indigent children, everyone knew it. Religious congregations stood as bulwarks against ignorance, illiteracy, disease, abandonment and secularism. We turned all our resources in those directions. Now, we have the best educated group of women in the world, each of whom is regarded with professional respect, and the most invisible congregations.

As our congregations decline in numbers of active members we can refocus our resources to insure that the gift of our corporate existence is not lost to the Church. That is a task for which we alone bear responsibility.

VIII. The Tutelle

A decade or longer before the vocation crisis was felt in the Church of the United States, the religious congregations of France had experienced decline and aging of membership. Still today, five million young people attend Catholic schools in France, most of which are congregational schools. In the great majority of these schools, the administration is lay and few religious are on staff.

With impetus and support from their leadership conference, the congregations of France, over the past eight to ten years, have developed the notion of the "tutelle." The service of the tutelle is to provide orientation to the educational mission of the congregation's schools, with emphasis on the distinctive characteristics of the congregation's educational philosophy and spirituality. Within congregations, meetings of lay and religious educators explore the values and goals of their common educational mission and tradition. Visitation, animation, and evaluation are responsibilities of the tutelle, which is exercised by the major superior and council of each congregation, following statutes for the tutelle that have been adopted on a national level.

In 1988 and again in April 1994, national convocations of French Catholic educators have attracted thousands of participants to an exchange on the experiences and development of the congregational tutelle.

The tutelle illustrates a clear way to structure the relationship between a congregation and its schools, made possible by a national collaborative effort under the leadership conference. Its merit is that the structure of the tutelle is simple and unambiguous. Whether a religious is in charge or not, it is the same. The benefit of adopting that structure is that it allows the energy of the congregation and of its lay collaborators to be channeled to the heart of their mission-effectiveness concerns, which is their common and primary goal. Congregations with their small numbers are re-engaged in a significant and in a visible way, bringing their particular gift to the Church.

The foregoing discussion, hopefully, will illustrate the ambiguity of sponsorship and provide some framework for the further discussion needed to develop clarity, so that ultimately we can direct more of our attention to the mission of our congregational apostolates.

Madeline Welch, O.S.U.

This article originally appeared in *Bulletin on Issues of Religious Law*, Vol. 10, 1994.

20.
CLERICS AND RELIGIOUS IN PUBLIC OFFICE: PROHIBITIONS IN CANON LAW

INTRODUCTION

The attempts of clerics to become actively involved in political affairs and to hold public office are not new. Through the centuries, there were repeated efforts by ecclesiastical authorities to formulate law in order to control the practice of priests who added to their spiritual ministry, for one reason or another, offices which were considered incompatible with the chosen vocation of the priesthood. Not only was this the stance of church authority, but secular rulers as well recognized that the mission of the cleric should be concerned primarily with spiritual matters and the salvation of souls.

Moreover, not only were the dignity of the clerical state and the purpose of the priestly vocation factors in the reasons behind the repeated prohibitions, there were also other objections which surfaced in time. Most of these objections were based on the belief that one person simply could not do justice to more than one major task in life. Another more serious objection was based on the fear that a portion of the liberty and discipline of the Church would be lost due to the fact that a cleric would necessarily become dependent upon those from whom he received temporal power. In addition, the good name of the Church and the ever-present possibility of liability against church property were always considerations behind the prohibitions.

From the time of the first instruction to Timothy, "In the army no soldier gets himself involved in civilian life because he must be at the disposal of the person who enlisted him (2 Tim 2:4)," the subject of the conduct of clerics with regard to involvement in secular affairs was dealt with in many early papal warnings, exhortations and decrees. In the early Church, local councils and synods frequently and emphatically addressed this matter.

The first universal law on this subject was enunciated in the Council of Chalcedon (451) in a broad prohibition. Canon 3 of this council decreed that no bishop, cleric or monk could become involved in the management of possessions and the administration of any kind of secular business. This law did offer the possibility for exceptions in particular situations, as in the service of a person in serious need. It was (and is) generally assumed that the laws regarding "public decorum" applied to clerical as well as to non-clerical women and men religious.

Subsequent councils stated in various ways — depending upon the times and circumstances — that it was not lawful for clerics to assume secular responsibilities, and harsh penalties were imposed. At times it was decreed that those who held certain secular offices must resign or be deposed, that is, lose their clerical functions. Lay persons who appointed clerics to offices of civil responsibility were to be excommunicated.

Much of the earlier legislation was concerned with the management of temporal goods. It was common in the first few centuries of the Church for wealthy lay persons to name clerics as executors of estates or as guardians of their children. Consequently, much of the time and interest of a cleric in such cases would be diverted to temporal matters. With the growth of the Roman Empire, much church legislation became concerned with clerics and religious holding positions in the imperial curia.

One must not omit mention of the *Decretum* of Gratian (1140), the first enduring systematization of all known church law. Clearly, the practice of clerical involvement in secular matters must have been rampant in Gratian's time, as evidenced by the inclusion of numerous references to past prohibitions against all unnecessary secular involvement. This trend, with precise adjustments from time to time, was repeated in all major legislation up to and including the 1917 and 1983 Codes.

Perhaps a statement which was sent to the committee in preparation for the Second Vatican Council best summarizes the concern of many in the Catholic community. The Ordinary of the Greek Armenian Church stated that it was not a rare event to see ecclesiastics who were not content to carry out their civic duty as they had been asked, that is, through writings and discussions against political parties which were opposed to the Church. Instead, they presented themselves as candidates in various elections. The danger of this activity is that such priests cannot do everything, and consequently they make enemies who also turn their hatred against the Church in general.

I. The 1917 Code

Church law over the centuries contained many references to the prohibition against clerics becoming entangled in secular affairs. However, few canons of the 1917 Code dealt directly with the matter of clerics as candidates for public office. Gasparri's *Codex iuris canonici*, promulgated under the authority of Pope Benedict XV, narrowed the number of norms and allowed exceptions born of long years of experience (canon 139).

It appears that it was the intention of the legislator that canon 139 not be comprehensive, but that it allow ordinaries to determine for their own regions which activities might be considered inappropriate for clerics. It was believed that the bishops might prohibit or allow activities according to the customs of the people.

A key section of this canon stated that clerics may not accept public offices which involve the exercise of lay jurisdiction or administration. Specifically mentioned were the offices of judge, mayor, governor, prefect of a province, president of a republic or similar offices.

Jurisdiction is defined as "the power of governing one's subjects through laws, decrees, mandates, precepts, sentences, etc." Administrative power is understood as the "ordinary direction of one's subjects, that is, the common and daily carrying out of the laws, particularly in certain and obvious cases where there is no dispute or contention." Public office as defined in the 1917 Code is a position of duty, trust or authority, especially in public service. Through the centuries the term *saecularia negotia* (secular occupations) came to mean anything, including civil office, which may remove a cleric from his sacred duties or corrupt him in any way.

A simple impediment to sacred orders was imposed on clerics who exercised any office or administration which required the rendering of an account. It is clear that the law attempted to avoid situations in which a cleric might jeopardize the Church because of past obligations he may have incurred. After the Edict of Milan (313) Constantine set the stage for the exemption of clerics from performing certain compulsory services which at the time were the responsibility of all citizens. Justinian's law of the mid-sixth century extended the prohibition further and expressed it more forcefully. These protections for the Church and its clergy were reflected in CIC canons 987, §3 and 121. It follows that most civil codes concede this favor of exemption to clerics in the present time as a special privilege to those who are actually engaged in ecclesiastical offices.

In summary, the 1917 Code followed the long tradition of the Church in safeguarding the dignity and spiritual mission of its clergy, and, perhaps just as importantly, endeavored to prevent situations from occurring which would encourage attacks by her enemies.

The code prohibited unnecessary involvement of clerics in legislative, administrative and judicial office. In short, they were precluded from activity in any secular or public office which would entail participation in the exercise of civil power or the rendering of an account.

There were exceptions to this general norm. With legitimate permission from the Apostolic See or the proper ordinary of place, individual clerics could engage in certain activities and accept certain political offices. The reasons for these exceptions had to be grave and to be for the good of the Church and its people.

Thus, it is clear that the official Church through its laws, as stated in the 1917 Code, has had a negative view of any public activity on the part of its clergy and religious. This traditionally firm stance has been borne out repeatedly in subsequent normative action and interpretation.

II. THE 1983 CODE

The traditional restriction on the political activity of clerics and religious, and in particular, on the holding of public office, did not diminish in the new code. The prohibition, in fact, became more restrictive as will be demonstrated in this section.

Adhering to the centuries-old tradition of admonitions against occupations, professions and activities which are considered unbecoming to the clerical and religious state, the 1983 Code essentially includes the canons on this subject in a general principle.

> Canon 285, §1 — In accord with the prescriptions of particular law, clerics are to refrain completely from all those things which are unbecoming to their state.

Since the promulgation of *Ministeria quaedam* in 1972 by Pope Paul VI, clerics are now defined as those ordained, that is, deacons, priests and bishops. Furthermore, according to the canons of this code, members of religious institutes (c. 672) and of societies of apostolic life (c. 739) are also bound by canon 285.

The 1983 Code omits the listing of the specific activities found in previous laws and leaves the ultimate determination of these activities to particular law, which in the mind of the legislator is in a better position to judge whether or not a certain activity may be suitable for a cleric or religious. Canon 285 offers a gradation of activities and offices which may be offensive to the clerical state, even if at times this may be contingent upon culture, traditions or circumstances.
Retained in the 1983 Code is the general norm:

> Canon 285, §2 — Clerics are to avoid those things which, although not unbecoming, are nevertheless alien to the clerical state.

This paragraph states that some professions and activities are worthy and good and are not debasing to the dignity of the clerical state nor unbecoming for lay persons to perform. They are, nevertheless, foreign to the clerical state and are judged as interfering with the spiritual mission of the ministry. It is clear that the provisions of former law remain and are retained in vigor and force in these canons.

> Canon 285, §3 — Clerics are forbidden to assume public offices which entail a participation in the exercise of civil power.

The force of this paragraph is far more restrictive than canons of former laws. The exhortative nature of former laws rendered a less forceful prohibition than that of the present code. The use of "public offices" (*civilis*) in this paragraph, rather than a list of particular offices, appears to narrow the sense of the exercise of power to whatever may be understood as public or political offices, which are positions of public trust and which carry with them an accountability to some form of government. Thus, the norm explicitly singles out and prohibits in a wider sense the exercise of civil power, that is, legislative, executive and judicial or, in other words, the taking on of any civic responsibility.

It also appears that the legislator was deliberately searching for an absolute formula of the prohibition without leaving open the means of making exceptions. The deliberate omission of the mention of the earlier exceptions, that is, the possibility of obtaining one by an apostolic indult or by permission from the ordinary or ordinary of place, precludes direct or unqualified access of clerics to public office.

Canon 285, §4 essentially repeats the norms of former law:

> Without the permission of their ordinary, clerics are neither to become agents for goods belonging to lay persons nor assume secular offices which entail an obligation to render accounts.

This section of the norm is concerned with clerics acting as agents for the temporal goods of lay persons. Generally, without the permission of their ordinary, clerics are not permitted to become guardians or executors of wills for lay persons. Authors believe that "secular offices" in this paragraph refer to whatever offices are involved with the economics of society whether for Catholics or non-Catholics.

The reasons for these restrictions are clear. There are obligations related to certain positions which carry with them the burden of rendering an account. These offices could become dangerous to both the individual cleric or religious and to the Church or religious congregation.

In the first case, a cleric or religious could potentially be called upon to devote an excessive amount of care for material goods; in the second, there would be economic risks incurred by ecclesiastical personnel which might involve the Church or congregations in liability. Therefore, the obvious intent behind the norm is to safeguard church personnel and property.

Just as important is the traditional intention to preserve the spiritual mission of the priesthood from entanglement in any secular affairs except the most necessary. It is left to the judgment of the ordinary and of major superiors to determine the circumstances for deciding when these may occur and when they may consider them to be legitimate.

Several canons of the new code are closely related to the prohibitions of canon 285.

Chapter IV of the section in the 1983 Code which contains obligations upon members of religious institutes states:

> Canon 672 — Religious are bound by the prescriptions of canons 277; 285; 286; 287; and 289, and, moreover, religious clerics are bound by the prescriptions of canon 279, §2; in lay institutes of pontifical right, the permission mentioned in canon 285, §4 can be granted by the proper major superior.

Canon 739 states that members of societies of apostolic life are bound by the common obligations of clerics. This canon is addressed only to clerical societies.

The following paragraph is a new norm and places a particular obligation on clerics. The reasoning was that this matter could be very important in the history of some nations in which clerics could not remain indifferent:

> Canon 287, §1 — Most especially, clerics are always to foster that peace and harmony based on justice which is to be preserved among all persons.

Canon 287, §1 sets the tone for the prohibitions mentioned in the second paragraph:

> Canon 287, §2 — Clerics are not to have an active role in political parties and in the direction of labor unions unless the need to protect the rights of the Church or to promote the common good requires it in the judgment of the competent ecclesiastical authority.

The canon places first a positive then a negative obligation on clerics. The first paragraph of the canon states that clerics are habitually to foster peace among all people, and not just any kind of peace, but that which is founded on justice. That is, they are required to do everything possible in defense of the rights of the human person when it deals with the demands of natural and positive justice. However, the correct fulfillment of this obligation does not presuppose an involvement in the affairs of the "earthly city," because the mission Christ gave to the Church had to do with religious order. Nevertheless, the Church by virtue of the gospels has been entrusted with proclaiming the rights of the people.

One commentary provides a salient reminder that the commitment of the cleric within the Christian community comes from his relationship to the bishop who is the principle and foundation and the visible sign of unity in the particular church. Therefore, the cleric should never be in the service of a certain ideology, but rather should be at the service of the body of Christ.

It appears from the wording of the canon that the law may allow membership in a party or union in circumstances where an active part would not be required and may provide for more freedom in this matter. In another canon (c. 288) it is stated that permanent deacons are not bound by canon 287, §2.

Canon 1042, 2° retains the simple impediment to sacred orders until the person aspiring to sacred orders becomes free of the position.

In keeping with ancient traditions, it is expected that civil governments will refrain from demanding official services from ministers. Canon 289, §2 obliges clerics to make use of these exemptions. Added to this canon, however, is the stipulation that, in particular cases, the proper ordinary may determine otherwise.

It is significant to note that a new norm, canon 275, §2, expresses the provisions of Vatican II, which places the responsibility for the building up of the temporal order with the laity. Clerics must take it as their obligation to acknowledge and promote that mission which lay persons exercise in their own way in the Church and in the world.

As restrictive as the formulation of the prohibitions in canon 285 at first appear, the law itself provides two major possibilities allowing for public offices and certain activities to be accessible to clerics, namely, dispensation and the judgment of the competent authority.

At times, there are circumstances, cultures, and traditions which appear to allow for a broader interpretation. This could leave room for exceptions to the general norm and to particular law. It is significant to note that the council fathers of Vatican II did not intend that clerics be entirely excluded from some involvement in secular affairs. The document *Gaudium et spes* 43 provides that clerics may be engaged in activities and professions which are not entirely of a spiritual nature.

When the new law was promulgated, there was no mention of the former requirement that bishops obtain permission from the Holy See to allow a cleric or religious to hold offices which require the exercise of civil power. Likewise, there was no mention of a pontifical reservation in places where there was a special prohibition, and no mention of specific situations in which an ordinary is competent to give permission for the exercise of civil power. Moreover, there is no mention of a circumstance when a cleric would need permission from the ordinary of place in connection with the soliciting or accepting of an elective office not in one's own diocese.

Because of these omissions and because of the unqualified prohibition in canon 285, §3, the only way a cleric or religious might hold public office is by obtaining a dispensation from the diocesan bishop. Canon 285, §4 provides that, after consulting with his ordinary, a cleric could manage his own goods and if necessary those of relatives, and may even assume the office of guardian or executor of a will with the proper permission.

A major requirement in the new code for freeing the cleric from the prohibition contained in canon 285, §3 is that of dispensation. (A dispensation is the relaxation of the law in a particular case.) Wider dispensing powers were given to diocesan bishops following Vatican II (see *Christus Dominus* 41, 8b). However, the diocesan bishop must be guided by the laws regarding the granting of dispensations, namely canon 90, §1 which states that the bishop must have sufficient cause (grave, just and rational) for granting a dispensation; and canon 90, §2 which states that when in doubt the dispensation granted by him is to be considered valid and licit.

In canon 287, §2 the law itself contains the possibility that clerics and religious may have an active role in politics and in the direction of labor unions, if, in the judgment of the competent authority, there is a need for a cleric to promote the common good or to defend the rights of the Church. This is not new in church law but follows early church tradition.

It is not clear in the law in such situations who the competent authority might be. It is thought that the authority to make such a judgment is the priest's own ordinary or the major superior in a religious congregation. In addition, though not specifically mentioned in the new law and in keeping with former norms, the judgment of the ordinary where the activity is to take place may also be sought.

If this authority finds that the conditions of the law as stated in canon 287, §2 are met, he may, in his judgment, consider that there are no legal objections to a request of a cleric to become involved in some political activity. Therefore, the law itself may allow a cleric to participate in politics or to hold leadership positions in a labor union in particular circumstances.

The current law does not express, as in former law, that clerics may not "solicit or accept" a legislative office or allow one's name to be placed as a candidate. Therefore, the law appears to allow a priest to run for an elective office which requires the exercise of civil power, providing the ordinary is satisfied that this is for the common good or the good of the Church. However, though the law allows for those possibilities, it is clear from canon 285, §3 that, if a cleric wins in a political race for public office, he may not assume that office without a dispensation from his ordinary.

It is to be noted that, since the prohibition is against only those offices which require the exercise of civil power, some offices though secular are not prohibited. Certain advisory positions or offices, such as advisors to a non-partisan citizen's group, to a president or to some other government official, are not prohibited.

Generally, a dispensation may be granted for some spiritual benefit and for the good of the faithful. However, in view of the current attitudes of the present Pope and of the Roman curia, it appears likely that diocesan bishops will be reluctant to grant the dispensations needed in the matter of priests and religious in public office except in the rarest of cases. Therefore, since it is more difficult to obtain a dispensation than a permission, it is evident that a more narrow determination is given in the new code regarding active involvement in political affairs.

III. Recent Applications

In "The Ministerial Priesthood" (Synod of Bishops, 1971), the matter of clerical involvement in secular and political activities was addressed. As a concise summary of the past and current church teaching, its statements on this topic would be a guide for bishops in the monitoring of the conduct of their clergy. "Secular activity should not become the principal objective of priests nor their responsibility. Activities of this kind belong primarily to lay persons. . ."

Probably the most significant expressions in our time of the stance of the Church concerning the political activity of clerics and religious were made in the years just prior to the promulgation of the new code by the supreme authority of the Church. Several of John Paul II's statements are based on the teachings of the Second Vatican Council.

In a major address to Latin American bishops in Puebla in January 1979, John Paul II attempted to place the mission of the Church in the world of temporal affairs. He stated that the Church's mission, though religious and not social or political, could not fail to consider all people in the entirety of their being. Yet, he was firm in denouncing political, revolutionary or violent approaches to the solution of social problems. It is clear that the Pope's public statement was an expression of his opposition to the political activity pursued by many of the Latin American clergy.

In a later address to priests in Mexico City, the Pope reminded them that they were "participants in the ministry of Christ for the service of the unity of the community" and that they should "observe an attitude of unity and obedience to their bishops." He reminded the priests on this occasion that they were "not social directors, political leaders or functionaries of a temporal power" and that "temporal leadership could easily become a source of division, while the priest should be a sign and factor of unity." The Holy Father made it clear that secular functions are the proper field of action of the laity.

On May 4, 1980, the Pope told the Zairean priests to "leave political responsibilities to those who are charged with them" and "to be mediators between God and man." He told them that they have a responsibility to help the laity to fulfill their role in the temporal order. The same firm message from John Paul II was passed on to religious priests in Sao Paolo in July 1980; in Manila in February 1981; and to the bishops of Nicaragua in June 1982.

As recently as July 28, 1993, the Pope, speaking before his weekly general audience, said that priests are called to work for peace and justice, but that they have "neither the mission nor the charism from on high" to get involved in political campaigns or movements.

Church authorities acting for the Pope intervened directly in two widely publicized cases in the United States. The first, in 1980, involved Father Robert Drinan, S.J., who had served for ten years in the U.S. House of Representatives. On April 27, 1980, Father Drinan received word through his provincial superior that the superior general of the Society of Jesus had directed him not to run for re-election. Later Father Drinan learned that the direction was the "express wish of John Paul II."

A second event in the United States involved Sister Agnes Mary Mansour, a Sister of Mercy from Michigan. Initially, with proper approval from the archbishop and from her religious superiors, Sister Agnes Mary accepted the position of Director of the Michigan Department of Social Services. A short time later the archbishop withdrew his approval, and on May 9, 1983, then Bishop Anthony Bevilaqua, delegated by Vatican officials, confronted Sister Agnes Mary with two choices. She was either to resign her position as director or be subject to a canonical process leading to imposed dismissal from the Sisters of Mercy. She chose instead to request a dispensation from her vows.

On March 8, 1982, the Sacred Congregation of the Clergy issued an instruction on associations of the clergy. The document was directed at priests' organizations in Hungary, Yugoslavia and Czechoslovakia. It stated that there was no room in the priestly ministry for organizations of a political nature which would "interfere with the service an ordained minister owed the faithful" and could "foster disunity among the faithful."

On December 4, 1984, Father Fernando Cardenal was dismissed from the Jesuit order for refusing to resign his government position in Nicaragua as education minister.

In March 1983 the Pope "wagged his finger publicly" at Father Ernesto Cardenal, brother of Fernando (both of Nicaragua), then minister of culture, showing his strong disapproval.

Although the Maryknoll Fathers refused to dismiss Father Miguel D'Escoto (Minister of Foreign Affairs for Nicaragua), the Vatican suspended him and, presently (as of September 1995), has refused to restore his priestly faculties, though he now works among the slum dwellers for a non-governmental organization.

The most recent case involves Father Jean-Bertrand Aristide of Haiti. Haiti's Catholic bishops have not supported Father Aristide's political endeavors. When the priest became involved in politics in 1988, he was expelled from the Salesian Fathers and has not served publicly as a priest since his election as president. Subsequently he has received a decree of laicization and a dispensation from vows.

These particular papal statements, examples of papal actions and documents from the Roman curia are mentioned to indicate the universality of the prohibitions. There appears to be no particular group or situation or country at which these repeated exhortations, warnings and instructions are aimed. There is a consistency in the restrictions as well as in the possibility of exceptions, and in the bases for the prohibitions. The norms in the 1983 Code reflect this firm and consistent stance of the universal Church.

For a more comprehensive study of this topic consult *Between God and Caesar: Priests, Sisters and Political Office in the United States*, edited by Madonna Kolbenschlag (New York: Paulist Press, 1985).

Claudia Barbre, R.S.M.

This article originally appeared in *Bulletin on Issues of Religious Law* Vol. 10, 1994.

III.
CONFIDENTIALITY

21.
THE ISSUE OF CONFIDENTIALITY IN RELIGIOUS LIFE

The recent history of humanity has been marked by an increased awareness of the rights of individuals. Indeed, the Second Vatican Council stated in the constitution *Gaudium et spes* 26: "There is a growing awareness of the exalted dignity proper to human persons, since they stand above all things, and their rights and duties are universal and inviolable." The 1983 Code of Canon Law shows that it is in tune with such sensitivity; however, as can be expected, the law does not enter into details regarding the way such rights are to be respected. It is satisfied with outlining a number of general principles, leaving the application to those charged with implementing the legislation.

One area in particular where this method was used is that of confidentiality. For, as it is well known, the issue is complicated somewhat by existing civil laws, which vary from place to place. Some of these laws seem to offer a general right to information, while others are more protective of confidentiality. Therefore, it follows that any statement of the Church's law would have to be complemented by a reference to the applicable civil legislation.

We shall address the issue of confidentiality first by looking at the general legislation; then by noting what the law for religious institutes states about the matter; and, finally, by making some practical applications to contemporary issues.

I. GENERAL PRINCIPLES

Canon 220 of the 1983 Code of Canon Law reads as follows: "No one is permitted to damage unlawfully the good reputation which another person enjoys nor to violate the right of another person to protect his or her privacy." This is taken from *Gaudium et spes* 26.

It can be noted that there are two parts to this canon: the right to one's reputation, and the right to privacy. We shall address each of these in turn.

A. THE RIGHT TO ONE'S REPUTATION
1. Loss of reputation

There are times when a person's reputation can be damaged lawfully, as is the case when a penal trial is held, a person is pronounced guilty, and the sentence is declared or the situation is notorious. But, as canon 1717, §2 provides, before the trial is held, "care must be taken lest anyone's good name be endangered by [the preliminary] investigation." Even after the trial, if the person cannot observe the penalty without danger of serious infamy, then the penalty is suspended for the time being (c. 1352, §2). Such cases, happily, are extremely rare in the Church today. In most other instances, any violation of someone's reputation is unlawful.

2. Harming a person's reputation

a. A reputation could be damaged first of all by revealing secrets. The highest form of secrecy is the seal of confession (cc. 983, §1; 1388, §1), binding on the confessor; parallel to this would be the committed secret, which binds those to whom confessional knowledge can come in any way (cc. 983, §2; 1388, §2).

But there are many other forms of secrecy mentioned in the code which are not as stringent: the secrecy of the proceedings of the marriage tribunal is one such instance (cf. c. 1455). Indeed, after speaking of the secrecy binding the judges and the tribunal personnel, canon 1455, §3 adds: "Moreover, as often as the nature of a case or the proofs is such that the reputation of others is endangered by divulging the acts or proofs, or an opportunity for discord is provided or scandal or some other similar disadvantage might arise, the judge can bind the witnesses, the experts, the parties and their advocates or proxies by oath to observe secrecy."

Canon 127, which speaks of the role of councils, has a similar prescription: "All whose consent or counsel is required are obliged to offer their opinion sincerely and, if the seriousness of the matter requires it, to observe secrecy sedulously, and this obligation can be insisted upon by the superior" (c. 127, §3).

There are other prescriptions regarding secrecy mentioned in canons 377, §3 (selection of bishops); 413, §1 (the person selected to govern the see when it is impeded); 489-490 (diocesan secret archives), and so forth.

The general norms of moral theology regarding the obligation of observing such secrecy would have to be observed in these and similar instances.

b. A second way in which a person's reputation could be violated would be through calumny and slander. Although these are not defined in the law, canon 1390, §2 provides that "One who ... injures the good reputation of another person can be punished with a just penalty, even including a censure" (such as excommunication). In other words, the law takes this obligation so seriously that a willful violation of a person's reputation could be subject to very severe penalties within the Church. If, unfortunately, such a violation were to occur, there always remains the obligation of making suitable reparation. Instances of calumny or slander could arise — and indeed such has been the case recently — when priests or teachers in Catholic schools are falsely denounced for actions they did not commit (particularly in matters of morals) or insinuations are made about their behavior without sufficient evidence or proof.

c. A third area concerns letters of recommendation. At times, we really have no choice — such letters have to be written or information provided in some other suitable manner. For instance, canon 241, §3 provides that "when persons seek admission after they have been dismissed from another seminary or from a religious institute, further testimony is required from their respective superior, especially regarding the cause of their dismissal or their leaving." If the reason for departure were public or of a public nature, such letters would have to be forthright, or at least should invite the recipient to have personal contact with the writer for additional information. At times, the refusal to write a letter of recommendation is sufficient indication in itself of a serious problem on the part of the candidate. But, if the information is strictly confidential or of the level of the internal forum, then it cannot be communicated, no matter how advantageous it would be to have access to it.

However, it must be noted that most problems around the application of canon 220 do not refer to protection of one's reputation. Those in administration are usually scrupulous in protecting the reputation of others, even at the risk of being severely criticized for doing so. It is more in the area of respect of privacy that the difficult situations arise today.

B. The right to privacy

The 1917 legislation did not spell out the right to privacy in the same way as the new code does. In fact, the previous code focussed more on the right to privacy in correspondence (cf. 1917 Code c. 611) than on other matters; the new law appears to extend the right to privacy to cover many personal issues.

But what are these specific areas to which the legislation applies? They would have to be deduced from experience and by analogy.

1. Probably the most evident cases arising today where the right to privacy is violated would be those instances where candidates to priesthood are forced to reveal their sexual orientation — something that seems very difficult to justify. The reason for adopting this policy was to avoid other difficulties later on, but the end does not justify the means used.

2. Another area would concern past medical history (e.g., cases of pregnancy, sexually transmitted diseases, and the like). A distinction would have to be made, evidently, between past illnesses which have no direct bearing on a candidate's aptitudes for religious life, and those which now affect a person's general health (e.g., an active case of AIDS).

3. A third area of concern would be that of having access to the results of the psychological assessment of candidates. During the preparatory period for the Code of Canon Law, the Commission (in 1981) approved the principle of psychological testing for candidates to priesthood. However, this prescription was not included specifically in the promulgated code in the section on seminaries (There is, nevertheless, an oblique reference to such testing in c. 642 for religious). But we must keep in mind that there is a major difference between having candidates undergo a psychological assessment, and having the results of such evaluation shared by many people.

4. A fourth area where respect of privacy intervenes concerns access to one's personal file, and the rights of persons who have written letters of recommendation in regard to a candidate. These rights must be studied in conjunction with the rights of individuals to have access in certain circumstances to their files. Yet, we must acknowledge that persons' rights to examine their files apply only to items that are of a public nature. Thus, if letters were requested under promise of secrecy (c. 645, §4), this promise has to be respected and the candidate should not be shown the correspondence. If necessary, such letters should be destroyed once they have served their immediate purpose. In a similar way, a candidate would not have a right to university transcripts that were issued with the proviso that they not be shown to the student. Nor would there be any right to know the detailed results of voting concerning a person's admission to vows or to orders. Finally, there would be no right to have access to letters denouncing a person if such letter were not used later on as the basis for an action. Of course, if there was ever a trial, the accused would have the right to know who the accusers are and what they are stating (c. 1720, 1° refers specifically to this). Privacy applies in both directions.

5. A fifth extension would be in the area of giving reasons for transfers, requests to depart from a seminary or institute, and so forth. A bishop is not always free to inform parishioners of the reasons for moving a parish priest, nor is the superior of a religious institute able to tell others why a certain member has decided to

leave the community. This approach is consistent with the underlying philosophy found in the new code. For, as we examine the law, we note a marked preference for personal governance, rather than for having authority shared by the group. The major reason for this approach lies in the protection of the right to privacy, because if decisions are to be taken by all, then they have to be informed of the details before making the decision. This could, at times, lead to a serious violation of privacy in very important matters (e.g., reasons for requesting a dispensation from vows, for sending a cleric or religious for therapy, for the refusal to admit to orders or vows, and so forth).

These general principles can now be applied more directly to the law governing religious institutes.

II. Privacy In Religious Institutes

Canon 642 is probably the principal canon in the law for religious dealing with protection of the right to privacy, although canon 618 also speaks of the "reverence" which superiors are to show for the human person.

Canon 642 is concerned with admissions to the institute. Three points are specifically mentioned in the canon as calling for verification: the health of the candidate, that person's character, and personal maturity. These three areas can be verified "if necessary by using experts, with due regard for the prescription of canon 220." The experts would be physicians, psychologists, counsellors, and the like. Each of these areas of inquiry could be considered in detail.

A. Health of the Candidate

Canon 642 speaks in general terms about a candidate's health. While it does not mention them specifically, there is no doubt that both physical and psychological health would have to be the object of an inquiry prior to admission. Canon 1029 on ordination states that candidates are to have "other physical and psychological qualities which are appropriate to the order to be received." By analogy, this could be applied elsewhere.

The same approach could be taken with canon 665 which speaks of absence from the institute for the purpose "of caring for poor health."

Verification of psychological health could not take place without the candidate's permission. Of course, since theoretically no institute is obliged to admit any candidate who applies, it could state that if a prospective candidate does not accept to undergo psychological evaluation, then the application will not be considered.

The problem arises, not so much on the level of taking the tests, but rather on who will have access to the results (with the candidate's permission) later on. In one institute of which I am aware, the members of the vocation team, the provincial superior and council, and the superior general and council all have access to such reports. This is obviously an abuse. For the immediate superior of the candidate (novitiate director, major superior, etc.) to be authorized to receive the report would be quite normal; to extend the permission beyond such people would require a proportionate reason. For instance, it might be understandable if the members of the formation team were to be authorized, but certainly not all the councilors.

B. Character

Evaluation of a person's character would have to take place within the context of the lifestyle of the institute. For instance, in a contemplative institute, greater stability would probably be required in a community that has a more stable type of apostolate (depending on the work to which that person has been assigned).

One of the points to be evaluated here — and this would not seem to be an invasion of privacy if handled with care — would be the candidate's family background. Persons who grew up in a family where alcoholism was a major problem, but where the situation was denied or hidden, or those who were victims of child sexual abuse, are not, as contemporary studies show, always able to cope with stressful situations in religious or community life. However, what often happens is that a person is not ready to admit that sexual abuse occurred in the past, particularly if it was on the part of members of the immediate family. It is probably in this area that formation personnel are coming face-to-face with situations that were not imagined in years gone by, or at least were not addressed. In the past, attention was placed more on mental illness in the family, or on specific medical histories (cardiac failure, cancer, etc.). It would seem that the focus should shift somewhat today, although it is evident that such information is much more sensitive than simple medical facts. If these points come to light, it would seem that they should not be documented in the candidate's file. Persons in authority would have a right to inquire about such situations, at least under the present legislation, but if such information is volunteered it should be carefully addressed.

C. Maturity

The third area that canon 642 mentions is "qualities of maturity to embrace the particular life of the institute." Therefore, as with personal character, a certain type of maturity could be required in one institute that would not be absolutely essential in another.

In addition to general maturity of judgment — which has long been the object of evaluation — we now note a special emphasis placed on affective maturity.

In marriage nullity cases, affective maturity would relate to the capacity of the person to love another. In consecrated life, this would apply to sexual maturity and integration, to the capacity to reach out to others, to love and be loved, according to the norms of religious life.

The experience of the marriage tribunal can indeed be helpful in this regard. It often happens that children who were the victims of family situations marked by divorce, infidelity, crime, and the like, are unable to trust. Something similar could be said about families that for generations have been on some type of social assistance. A religious who would be unable to trust would not be capable of entering into the positive dynamics of community life, or could do so only with great difficulty. My personal experience in seminary formation work also reveals that candidates who were police officers or those who were the only child are usually very difficult candidates in this regard.

There is no doubt that such information might come to light during the admissions process, since many of the facts are of a public nature, although, of course, the individual's reactions to these facts can vary significantly from person to person. But, if it is not volunteered, it does not seem that those conducting the inquiry would have a right to delve too deeply into the matter.

The other points in the law for religious governing the respect of privacy will be reviewed in the following section.

III. Practical Applications

While the principles outlined above seem to be rather clear, they are liable to divergent interpretations. A few of the practical applications can now be mentioned.

A. Custody of personal files

1. In many civil jurisdictions, the concept of "secret archives" is no longer recognized. Thus, it follows that documents contained in the personal file of a religious might be subject to subpoena by the civil courts. For this reason, it would seem that documentation that could be derogatory to a person's reputation should not be kept in that person's file. Or, as a minimum, canon 489, §1 should be applied with the necessary adaptations: "Every year documents of criminal cases are to be destroyed in matters of morals in which the criminal has died or in which ten years have passed since the condemnatory sentence; but a brief summary of the case with the text of the definitive sentence is to be retained."

It is evident that in most instances there is no criminal trial in church courts, and therefore there is no definitive sentence. However, it could be recommended that documents relating to moral issues should not be kept unless it is absolutely necessary to do so for other reasons (e.g., an eventual dismissal case). A superior is always free to keep personal files, distinct from the members' regular files, but, again, such personal files would generally not be considered to be privileged in all civil jurisdictions. (It is possible that in the United States the first amendment could be invoked successfully in some instances as has been the practice when the files of the marriage tribunals were subpoenaed by the civil courts).

2. When psychological assessment reports are available, it should be remembered that these retain their validity only for a given period of time. Therefore, it seems that these documents should also be destroyed once they have served their immediate purpose. Although the candidate is usually given the substance of the report, and at times even a copy of the document itself, at other times only parts are directly communicated (with that individual's consent) to the person being evaluated. There are sometimes elements contained therein that a person is unable to handle adequately (e.g., a lack of judgment). Individuals who would have access to their personal files might suffer more damage than good from reading them if the documents could not be interpreted correctly.

B. Transmission of sensitive information

1. Major superiors have a right to be informed of their candidates' progress, but even they do not have a right to know everything that a candidate has revealed to others, particularly to a spiritual director who might also happen to be a formation director. Canon 240, §2 provides that "in making decisions concerning the admission of students to orders or their dismissal from the seminary, the opinion of the spiritual director and the confessors can never be sought." With the necessary adaptations, this same canon should be applied to religious institutes, even in those instances where the spiritual director is not a priest bound by the seal of confession.

2. Also, canon 630, §5 should be kept in mind: "Members are to approach superiors with trust, to whom they can express their minds freely and willingly. However, superiors are forbidden to induce their subjects in any way to make a manifestation of conscience to them."

For this reason, there should be clear parameters established when a superior (formation director, etc.) is conversing with a candidate. It should be made evident to the person whether or not the information imparted will be eventually used in reaching a decision regarding that candidate's suitability for the specific vocation in question.

C. Transfer of religious

In the cases of transfers from one religious institute to another, the rights of all persons involved are to be respected. While the individual religious certainly has a right to privacy at this moment, the receiving institute would also have a right to objective information concerning the person who is transferring. Such information should not go into great details — this would be left to the individual to communicate to the new institute — but public or well-known facts should in all honesty be brought to the attention of the receiving institute, if not in writing, at least orally. It would seem that the personal file of a candidate, or at least the documents that are still relevant, could be given to the new institute (with the person's consent).

Again, however, matters of conscience that the superior might know through personal contact should not be communicated without the candidate's express permission.

Sometimes, a note of caution to the receiving institute is sufficient. Yet, at times, even this might be suspect because of some type of personality conflict between the religious and the superior, although this excuse should not be used too readily.

It would seem that the presumption would be in favor of the superior's judgment.

D. Previous treatment

1. If a candidate for a transfer (to another institute, or even to another province of the same institute) had been in therapy for an extended period of time for substance abuse (alcohol, pharmaceutical products) or for psychological problems, in all honesty reference would have to be made to this fact — without entering into all the details. If it were simply a passing episode, rather than a personality pattern, a prudential judgment would determine how much information if any was to be given. It does not seem that the superiors should transmit intimate personal details, but they would have the right — and perhaps even the obligation — to mention that there were problems in the past.

2. If the candidate has a communicable disease, or one that will undermine health seriously in the years ahead, it seems that the new community should be informed.

If a person were to carry AIDS anti-bodies (but was not an active AIDS victim), such a person would not have to inform the superior of the situation, and so it follows that the superior of the institute a person is leaving should not communicate this information to the new institute if it were known. It would be different if the person were an AIDS victim or had some similar illness.

E. Right of superiors to receive information

1. Since many institutes are sending their members for extensive therapy at specialized clinics or centers, and since in many instances they are disbursing substantial sums for such assistance, it follows that they should have some right to information regard-

ing the patient's progress.

It would seem that the best way for this to occur is for the patient to sign a release authorizing the treating physician or the counsellor to communicate with the superior, at times, in the presence of all three persons together.

But if the patient does not authorize such communication, it would seem that there is no right to information to any extent other than immediate family members would receive from a doctor. Much would depend on the treating physician or counsellor.

Respect of privacy would even apply, it seems, to the very fact that a member is obliged to seek therapy or counselling.

2. It is evident that the vow of obedience cannot be invoked in order to force a patient to recover from an illness, but in some instances it has been used as a last resort in bringing a candidate to make a decision as to whether or not to accept therapy. But there is a difference between obliging a person to seek help and forcing that person to cooperate with the authorities of the clinic during the period of treatment. However, it must be remembered that if a person is really sick, the less possibility there is of invoking the vow, particularly if a dismissal process were to ensue. (This is one of the weaknesses of the new code: superiors have very few means available whereby they can oblige a member to seek for and obtain available and necessary medical or psychological assistance.)

Conclusion

It is evident that we are dealing with a new dimension in law. The individual religious certainly has rights, and these cannot be overlooked. But we must not forget that the institute and the church as a whole also have rights.

The tension between the two sets of rights has come to the fore recently with the rash of cases involving pedophilia. A priest (diocesan or religious) cannot simply be suspended because there is an accusation against him, nor, on the other hand, can he be expelled from the clerical state if he is incapable of committing an imputable crime. The legislation as it stands is obviously inadequate; however, with time there will be established a jurisprudence or *stylus curiae* (cf. c. 19) that will enable us to operate efficiently in such delicate matters.

As it stands, the law is on the side of the individual and not enough on the side of the institute once a candidate has made perpetual profession. Therefore, as a practical norm of action, it could be stated that if a superior is to err at this time, it would seem preferable to err on the side of the member, protecting the rights to privacy and to one's reputation, leaving it up to the member to take any other necessary steps.

We have come a long way since *Gaudium et spes* 26 proclaimed the right "to a good reputation" and to the "protection of privacy." The Council went on to state that "the social order and its development must unceasingly work to the benefit of the human person if the disposition of affairs is to be subordinate to the personal realm and not contrariwise, as the Lord indicated" (ibid.). We are seeing the implications of the revised legislation incorporating these rights and spelling them out in practical terms. In the years ahead it is possible that new situations will have to be addressed, and it is also possible that the pendulum will shift somewhat to provide protection also for the institute and the Church as a whole when certain matters pertaining to privacy are considered.

Francis G. Morrisey, O.M.I.

This article originally appeared in *Bulletin on Issues of Religious Law*, Vol.4, 1988.

22.
CONFIDENTIALITY ISSUES REGARDING A RELIGIOUS INSTITUTE AND ITS RELATIONSHIPS WITH A DIOCESE

INTRODUCTION

Contemporary ecclesial governance is to be marked by a concern for the protection of rights, not the least of which are confidentiality and the protection of the reputation of those persons who serve the Church. Indeed, this is recognized as an essential element of any authentic form of contemporary governance. To act otherwise would be to betray the office. However, when it comes to addressing certain sensitive issues, such as financial mismanagement, there is a risk that only this particular issue be taken into consideration at the time, and that limitations in regard to confidentiality are overlooked.

One other such significant issue today is sexual misconduct, more particularly the sexual abuse of minors and of vulnerable adults perpetrated by pastoral workers. The issue has to be addressed squarely and openly. But at the same time, the norms regarding confidentiality and respect of persons have also to be kept in mind and observed. For instance, there is a difference between informing a bishop of certain aspects of a person's past and informing the entire parish congregation of the same.

Given the fact that many types of sexual dysfunction, as well as certain addictive forms of behavior, can be successfully treated today, it would be important for a person who is presented for pastoral services to have addressed beforehand any of these issues so that those who are being served will not become potential targets for the pastoral worker.

While much publicity has been given to the cases of priests and brothers, we cannot overlook the situation of women religious as well as of other pastoral workers. They too are exposed to similar illnesses and lapses.

In particular today, when religious men and women are being presented to a diocesan bishop for a pastoral assignment in the diocese, it can be asked whether the bishop has the right — and even the obligation — to know everything about that religious' past. Sometimes it is preferable to know less than more. Can the bishop insist, for instance, on total revelation of a person's past before a ministry is entrusted to a religious? These are some of the questions to be addressed in this brief study. Since the questions are new, so too will be the answers. This means that they are not — and cannot be — definitive. However, they can serve as indications given to those in positions of authority, showing how to proceed in a responsible and respectful manner when such issues arise.

I. Confidentiality

A number of issues are related to the question of confidentiality. In particular, three of them can be addressed here: the right to one's reputation, the right to privacy, and the obligations of superiors in this area.

A. The Right to One's Reputation

Canon 220 prescribes that "no one is permitted to damage unlawfully the good reputation which another person enjoys . . . " This presupposes that there are certain lawful ways in which a person's reputation can be damaged; the most obvious of these being the sentence of excommunication (or something similar) handed down after a penal trial in the Church. But even in such processes, there are provisions in the law to "take care lest anyone's good name be endangered" (c. 1717, §2). To show how seriously this obligation is taken, canon 1390, §2 provides that one who injures the good reputation of another person can be punished with a just penalty, including a censure. Therefore, there is no doubt that there are limits as to what can be communicated about one person to another without that person's consent.

A second point could be kept in mind. There is a difference between certain past situations and present ones. It is possible that in some distant past a religious was in trouble. The issue was subsequently addressed and is completely under control. Is it necessary for all the past to be brought up each time a religious is presented for assignment in another diocese? It would seem not. Just as there are certain statutes of limitation in canon law for offenses (see c. 1362) — five years for cases of sexual misconduct — so too should there be some limits placed on the communication of past experiences.

B. The Right to Privacy

Canon 220 also provides that "no one is permitted [. . .] to violate the right of another person to protect his or her own privacy." This means that even a religious major superior does not have the right to know everything about a member of the institute. Indeed, canon 630, §5 states that "superiors are forbidden to induce their subjects in any way whatever to make a manifestation of conscience to them."

The situation is different, of course, if the religious spontaneously wishes to reveal matters to the superior. For instance, a religious who has been in residential therapy authorizes the superior (and the superior alone) to receive regular progress and discharge reports from the center. These reports should not be kept indefinitely in the files; they are personal documents addressed to the superior. For this reason, they should be destroyed after a certain period of time, perhaps keeping, as canon 489, §2 provides in another context, "a brief summary of the case" and possibly the recommendations from the discharge report for after-care and on-going support.

While this is true in general, there are certain limitations to the application of the principle. For example, some civil jurisdictions now have regulations that require any person applying for employment in a field that entails contact with the public to state in writing whether in the past there have been accusations of sexual misconduct, and if so, under what circumstances. Certain diocesan regulations require compliance with these prescriptions. These regulations are attempting to eradicate from society (civil and religious) the plague of sexual abuse of minors. Therefore, at this time, it might be necessary to keep such statutes and policies in mind where they are in effect. However, the civil statutes usually concern the person applying for a position, not the superior who presents that person.

Also, we could keep in mind that when informing a person who needs to know about someone's past, it is usually sufficient to inform that person about the general nature of the situation or the offense, not all the details.

C. Particular Obligations of Superiors Relating to Confidentiality

One of the major obligations of superiors is to carry out their duties "with reverence for the human person" (c. 618). They are also to promote working together "for the good of the institute and of the Church" (c. 618). This can have many dimensions.

For instance, just as with physical persons, so too with juridical persons: their reputation is to be protected. Therefore, a superior could not in good conscience present for an assignment outside the institute a person who would seriously risk damaging the good name of the community and hinder future harmonious relations between the institute and the diocesan authorities.

If issues of sexual misconduct have arisen in the past, the superior would have to make a prudential judgment as to whether or not these have been addressed in a satisfactory manner, or whether there still remains a serious on-going risk. Given the contemporary situation, it would seem that at this time the good of the Church as a whole would prevail over the individual's right to privacy and intimacy. Indeed, canon 223 tells us that in exercising rights, we "must take account of the common good of the Church and of the rights of others as well as [our] own duties towards others." Therefore, there are certain things that must be communicated to diocesan authorities, while other matters are to be treated as strictly confidential. We shall examine some of these momentarily. But before doing so, it would be important to review some of the responsibilities of bishops and major superiors in relation to the placement of religious.

II. Responsibilities of Bishops and Major Superiors in Relation to the Assignment Of Religious

A. Diocesan Bishops

One of the first duties of a diocesan bishop, and of those who share intimately in his office of governance, is to promote the well-being of the particular church entrusted to his care, fostering various aspects of the apostolate, urging the observance of all ecclesiastical laws (see cc. 394, §1 and 392, §1).

Therefore, before appointing a priest as parish priest, the bishop is to make certain that this person "is distinguished for his sound doctrine and integrity of morals" (c. 521, §2). By analogy, the same principles could apply to all religious who are to be given a pastoral assignment.

If someone is obviously unworthy, it would be completely wrong on the part of the diocese to assign that person to ministry until the situation has been addressed. Therefore, a religious who is addicted to alcohol or other drugs would be expected to undergo treatment and satisfactory on-going aftercare before being assigned. The same could be said, and even more strongly, in the case of a religious involved in sexual abuse of minors.

Furthermore, canon 678, §3 provides that "in organizing the works of the apostolate of religious, it is necessary that diocesan bishops and religious superiors proceed after consultation with each other." The canon does not spell out the object of such consultation, but the qualifications of a person could certainly be part of the consultative process of assignment.

At the same time, though, we must not forget that religious institutes, by law, have "a rightful autonomy of life" (c. 586, §1) which local ordinaries are bound to safeguard and protect (see c. 586, §2). One way of upholding the autonomy of an institute is for the diocesan bishop to rely on the word of the major superior.

B. Religious Major Superiors

Just as a diocesan bishop has certain obligations, so too do major superiors.

Probably their first obligation in this area would be to present for assignment only those religious who are known (in the external forum) to be worthy of an appointment. To do otherwise would be unfair to all concerned: the diocese, the institute, the religious in question, and those who are to benefit from the ministry.

Since treatment on a residential or out-patient basis is readily available today to help remedy many situations, there would be a responsibility on the part of superiors to make certain that such possibilities are offered to the religious. Of course, a religious cannot really be forced to go to treatment, but any eventual assignment would depend on the successful completion of the therapy. Since such services, though, can be somewhat expensive, a just discretion of judgment would be needed to determine when such assistance could be beneficial. (A religious certainly does not have the right to remain in therapy indefinitely.)

Just as the diocesan bishop has to protect the autonomy of an institute, so too do superiors have to be watchful lest this autonomy be eroded by various encroachments. For this reason, "mutual consultation" could also take place regarding this aspect of the superior's duties.

III. Means of Protecting the Rights Of All Concerned

Recently, a number of means have been considered to see how these mutual and sometimes conflicting obligations can be carried out responsibly. Probably not all the proposed means — particularly those that saw the matter entirely in a civil law perspective, such as certain "hold harmless agreements" — have sufficiently respected the underlying canonical legislation. We can now look at one possible way that attempts to reconcile as many issues as possible.

A. A Statement from the Major Superior

When the issue of pedophilia began to surface, shock waves moved through the Church in North America. Not only were there extremely serious moral and societal issues, but also the financial implications were frightening.

In order to protect dioceses from certain forms of litigation and liability issues, it was thought in some places that all responsibility should be placed on the religious institute if the person involved in pedophilia was a religious. However, the matter was not that simple. Canon 681, §2 provides that there be a written agreement drawn up between the diocesan bishop and the competent superior of the institute, describing the relationships that are to exist between the two. In many such agreements, the issues of agency and liability have been addressed, distinguishing between what a religious does on the occasion or in virtue of a pastoral assignment, and what that person does in other times. It should be remembered that if a diocese wishes to benefit from the services of religious or of other pastoral agents, it also has to assume some of the ensuing responsibilities (and even liabilities).

Some dioceses wanted the major superiors to sign agreements that would operate in the sphere of civil law. However, after due consideration, is was considered — and rightly so — preferable to proceed "in a pastoral and canonical" manner, rather than running the risk of complicating litigation before the courts rather than simplifying it.

After much discussion in various places with diocesan bishops, religious major superiors, civil lawyers and canonists, it was agreed that four elements could be used for a statement to be issued by the major superior concerning the past and the present. As regards the future — after an assignment is made — the agreement between the diocese and the institute would apply. These four elements would respect confidentiality, but at the same time ensure that the bishop received sufficient information regarding the person presented to him:

> 1) First of all, any information to be communicated is to be based exclusively on matters relating to the external forum;
>
> 2) The superior's testimonial would mention that the religious is of good character and reputation. At one point, it was thought that a statement could also be made to the effect that the religious had not been subject to any penal processes in the Church and was not under any censure. However, this approach was abandoned since so few persons have been the subject of such procedures;
>
> 3) That the superior is unaware of anything in the person's background making such a religious unsuitable to work with children. It is a fact, though, that such situations are sometimes deeply hidden and the superior is one of the last persons to become informed of what is happening;
>
> 4) That the superior has no knowledge that the religious has a current, untreated alcohol or substance abuse problem. As various possibilities were considered, it was asked whether it was appropriate to state that a religious has been (or has not been) in therapy since not every person wants this fact disclosed and there is no specific need to do so. What counts is that a situation that required treatment has been addressed. It is presumed, then, that no mention need be made of this fact.

The religious in question should receive a copy of the letter or statement sent to the bishop.

One additional factor to be kept in mind when considering such a statement is that superiors change regularly and are usually not informed by their predecessors of all the details relating to the members' past.

B. Acceptance by the Diocesan Bishop

A bishop who would receive a statement or letter to this effect from the major superior would certainly be deemed to be acting responsibly from a canonical perspective in assigning the religious to ministry. Obviously, the superior would be responsible for the veracity of the statements.

This entails, however, an attitude of mutual trust and respect. But it goes even further: it also demonstrates respect for the persons directly involved.

In issuing a statement such as the one described above, confidentiality is preserved to the extent that is necessary, yet at the same time, diocesan authorities are given sufficient facts upon which to base a prudent decision.

C. Preservation of Records in Archives

One side issue that has arisen recently in cases involving dioceses and religious institutes is that of availability of documents and records. Generally speaking, in North America, such documents are not considered privileged by the secular courts, even though used exclusively for church purposes. Whether they will be seized or not is another question. However, on a number of occasions, church records have been the object of court subpoenas — even in the case of those kept in the secret archives. Therefore, it would be of great importance to make certain that documents are not kept in the archives — general or secret — which would severely damage a person's reputation, unless such matters have already become public. The archives should keep only that which is necessary for good governance, destroying periodically that which does not need to be kept for purposes of history.

Conclusion

It is still too soon to determine whether a statement from major superiors incorporating the four points mentioned above will be sufficient to protect dioceses from liability in the civil sphere. It is certainly hoped so. To go beyond that type of disclosure would appear to be in violation of a number of rights and obligations: the rights of the individual to privacy and to reputation, the rights and responsibilities of the major superiors relating to their members and to the protection of the autonomy of the institute, the duties of the diocesan bishop relating to pastoral assignments.

It would seem appropriate, then, for major superiors to ask diocesan bishops whether they would be satisfied with such a statement when a religious is presented for assignment. It certainly seems to meet the requirements of canon law; it is pastorally responsible; it respects the integrity and autonomy of institutes; yet it takes into account the responsibilities of bishops for their churches and for the well-being of the entire People of God.

Hopefully, before too long, the plague of child sexual abuse will be eradicated from society and the need for such statements will have disappeared.

Francis G. Morrisey, O.M.I.

This article originally appeared in *Bulletin on Issues of Religious Law*, Vol. 7, 1991.

23.
THE INDIVIDUAL'S RIGHT TO CONFIDENTIALITY

INTRODUCTION

Confidential material is that which is held in confidence or in secret. It may or may not be shared with another. It is private and, according to the dictionary, belongs to oneself and not to any public entity.

Once confidential material is known by a second or third party, the individual begins a journey on a very narrow winding road between the right to privacy and the wider community's welfare, or the common good.

Previous entries in this collection have considered confidentiality within religious institutes and between religious institutes and dioceses. This article will consider various aspects of confidentiality as it applies to individual members of religious institutes: the right itself, its limitations, and certain special situations in which the narrow winding road which forms the boundary between the individual's right and the welfare of the community is negotiated.

I. THE RIGHT TO CONFIDENTIALITY IN CANON LAW

Canon law does not, per se, guarantee a right of confidentiality to individuals. However, the law does present a number of stipulations from which such a right might be inferred. For instance, canon law acknowledges for every member of the Christian faithful "the right ... to protect his or her own privacy" (c. 220). The right is not presented absolutely for each individual, but as part of an injunction never to violate another's right to privacy nor unlawfully damage his or her good name (c. 220). Since no one may violate another's right to privacy, it can be assumed that each individual has the right, as well as the right to one's good name.

Canon 220 is rooted in the foundational teaching of Vatican II on the dignity of the human person as articulated in *Gaudium et spes* 26 and 27.

Accompanying and complementing the canonical principle of the dignity of the human person, and further clarifying any claims an individual in religious life might make to confidentiality, the following stipulations can be considered: religious superiors are to exercise their authority "with reverence for the human person" (c. 618); and superiors are always to respect an individual's freedom of conscience with regard to the sacrament of penance and spiritual direction (c. 630, §5). Thus, in any dealings with superiors, an individual religious may justifiably have the expectation of being treated with reverence. He or she can also expect privacy in conscience and spiritual matters.

The law has further stipulations which illustrate the connection between dignity of the person and confidentiality. In cases where accusations have been made against an individual, care must be taken lest during the investigation the person's good name is harmed (c. 1717, §2). Also, those who accuse falsely are to be punished for their actions (c. 1390, §2).

Even when offenses are committed, the guilty party is entitled, in the law, to reclaim his or her good name. For certain canonical offenses there is a statute of limitations for punishment (c. 1362); and diocesan secret archives, where incriminating materials are kept, are to be updated once a year and unnecessary materials discarded (c. 489, §2).

Taking all these points together, we get a general framework within which an individual's claim to confidentiality begins to take shape; it is a framework which stands on the foundational point of the dignity and value of each person and then extends to reverence, freedom from invasion of conscience, protection when under accusation, and protection from false accusations.

II. LIMITATIONS ON THE RIGHTS OF THE INDIVIDUAL

No canonical rights are absolute under all circumstances. They are held and exercised only in balance with obligations or with the rights of others and the common good.

> In exercising their rights the Christian faithful, both as individuals and when gathered in associations, must take account of the common good of the Church and of the rights of others as well as their own duties towards others.
>
> In the interest of the common good, ecclesiastical authority has the competence to regulate the exercise of the rights which belong to the Christian faithful (c. 223).

The term "common good" has a rich history, but its meaning is made quite clear in the documents of Vatican II. It is:

> ... the sum of those conditions of social life which allow social groups and their individual members relatively thorough and ready access to their own fulfillment (*Gaudium et spes*, 26).

In other words, to say that in the Church individual rights are always limited by the common good sets up a living, breathing dynamic which has some clear boundaries, but also points of intersection which call for sensitivity, negotiation, discretion.

Because the needs of the common good are interpreted by individuals differently at different times, and because ecclesiastical authority may be within or without a religious institute, difficulties and conflicts often arise. The possibilities for conflict are too numerous to mention, and are limited only by the variety of individuals in religious life. Here, four situations of dynamic tension between the individual's right to privacy and the needs of the common good will be considered: mental health records, medical records, personnel files and employment recommendations.

III. Specific Situations

In law applying specifically to members of religious institutes, there are requirements for documentation of suitable "health, character and maturity" as part of the admission process for the institute (c. 642). Institutes are given further leeway to inquire about candidates for admission, if such investigation seems called for, even to the point of making secret inquiries (c. 645, §4). This, of course, opens the door to letters of recommendation, psychological and medical testing and the handling of these confidential materials.

A. Mental Health Records

The individual seeking admission to the institute has rights in this situation which the institute, acting out of a sense of reverence and respect for the individual, is obliged to make known. Ideally, the individual is aware of the realities of the "balance of rights" as these now exist in the Church; if necessary, he or she is informed of the delicate nature of the results of psychological testing and has on hand the written policies of the institute concerning how those results are made available to formation or other personnel of the institute. The individual is informed of where these reports are kept, what persons have access to them and for what period of time. All these steps are in keeping with and respect an individual's right to privacy, while at the same time give some parameters to the responsibility of authority to preserve the common good.

When the need is indicated, those professed or incorporated religious who receive counseling/therapy, because of the institute's respect and reverence for them, are also informed of their right to privacy with respect to records from their treatment. For instance, an individual religious might want to know how billing and insurance forms are processed within the institute and what personnel have access to information, especially diagnoses, from them.

Surely, the individual psychologist informs every client of the ethical standards of confidentiality imposed on them by professional societies such as the American Psychological Association: the need for signed consent forms from the one tested or treated to release information to an institute or to allow consultation with superiors; the responsibility of the therapist to maintain confidentiality unless prohibited by law from doing so (for example, in situations of abuse, potential harm or the planned commission of a crime.) Although law and practice vary from state to state, in some situations it would be beneficial for the client to know that the records of a therapist can be subpoenaed in civil court and must be released under pain of contempt charges.

Certainly, the primary responsibility for knowing one's rights lies with the individual, but justice dictates that an institute or other ecclesiastical body provide information if necessary. Unless a given individual is aware of these points on the right to privacy/confidentiality, he or she may be unjustly deprived of the right or may presume protection from it when no protection is actually available.

B. Medical Records

For some individuals the concern might be for the confidentiality of medical records rather than psychological records. Here, too, that individual is wise who knows his or her own rights, the balance of rights as they are in the Church and the ethical expectations placed on physicians by their own profession to guard the privacy of their patients.

In general, despite differences from state to state, federal laws protect the confidentiality of medical records, and information may not be disclosed without "the patient's consent documented in writing by a special authorization form signed by the patient or the patient's legal representative." Patient information concerning a number of areas, among them substance abuse treatment and HIV testing, are often subject to more stringent regulations on confidentiality. Physician violation of disclosure laws which result in patient harm or injury are actionable in court. In some states these violations are punishable as misdemeanors.

If HIV or AIDS testing is a mandatory part of an institute's admission process, the candidate willingly agrees to the testing to achieve the desired goal; but the candidate should know beforehand how his or her right to privacy will be respected once the results are obtained. The candidate should clearly understand the role of these test results in the overall admission process.

An individual does not abdicate any aspect of the civil right to privacy and confidentiality by incorporation into a religious institute. The individual willingly accepts the limitations associated with the canonical right for the sake of the common good, but hopefully not without complete initial understanding of what the right entails.

C. Personnel Files

What are the reasonable expectations of the individual religious for privacy with respect to personnel files? The law of the Church does not offer specifics on this matter for religious institutes; thus, the individual's reasonable expectations are framed by particular law, policies and practice.

The responsibilities of superiors in this matter have been outlined elsewhere but the concomitant right of the individual requires a clear articulation of the institute's law, policies and practice.

For instance, an individual who at one time allowed confidential medical or psychological reports to be released to a specific superior is justified in asking what happens to the report when a new superior is elected. (The inquiry is particularly crucial in the absence of any written policies on such matters.) As mentioned earlier, there is an expectation in the law that confidential diocesan files are culled and unnecessary or outdated incriminating documents destroyed once a year (c. 489, §2). If such a procedure were in place for personnel files in religious institutes, a person with a past, so to speak, might have legitimate hope for an unclouded future.

The disposition of written documents concerning issues such as labor disputes, ministry complaints, or former substance abuse situations are also the subject of legitimate inquiry by the individual religious. It is well documented that diocesan personnel files, although they have some protection under canon and civil law, are vulnerable to subpoena. By analogy, the personnel files of religious institutes are also protected yet vulnerable. That fact, plus the litigious tenor of our times, makes the content and handling of one's personnel file a point of concern.

In summary on this subject of personnel files, an individual religious, under the banner of the canonical right to privacy and to one's good name, is entitled to know what is kept in his or her file and how that material is handled. Superiors, under the banner of reverence for the individual and care for the common good, create, maintain and administer these files in a spirit of discretion, justice and charity.

D. Letters of Recommendation

In November 1993, the NCCB approved a document called "Proposed Guidelines on the Assessment of Clergy and Religious for Assignment." The guidelines are recommended for use between bishops and major superiors as the "consistent approach … to share necessary information, candidly and confidentially, about candidates" for employment/ministry (p. 2). According to the guidelines, the sending bishop or major superior reviews the written records of the candidate's past employment and makes appropriate inquiries at past assignments. This information forms the foundation of the assessment which, in addition to evaluating fitness for the proposed assignment, goes on to reflect "whether the candidate has exhibited seriously improper behavior such as an untreated problem with substance abuse, violations of celibacy, sexual impropriety, physical abuse or financial impropriety" (p. 5). The individual's right to privacy was clearly a concern for the framers of these guidelines, as was the common good. Thus, "all communications … under these guidelines are confidential, to protect both the candidate and the providers of information. … Matters disclosed in the final statement should have been previously communicated to the candidate" (p. 5).

A sample "Letter/Statement on the Suitability of a Candidate" is provided along with the text of the guidelines (p. 8), and "(f)ailure to provide such a statement is sufficient reason for delaying or denying appointment to a candidate" (p. 5).

In this document we see the narrow winding road between rights being traveled. The individual has the right to privacy, but those to be served have a right to protection from harm. The individual who has the potential to harm must cede to the common good. The injunction of the law is that no one unlawfully harm the good name of another. Thus, there are circumstances in which the truth must be told and a good name lawfully harmed, so to speak. Will these guidelines eliminate all potential for injustice against individuals? Certainly not. Nor will every wider community be protected from harm. But this document is an attempt at negotiating that very delicate territory.

It is unfortunate that the guidelines are not more strongly worded on the responsibility of the sending bishop/major superior to communicate the content of the assessment to the candidate. Since the expectation of the communication is stated, surely the candidate is free to request a copy of the document, should these guidelines be operative in the given situation. Of course, as the guidelines indicate, the sending bishop/major superior always has the option of remaining silent, sending no assessment.

In this process, as in any other personnel issue, that individual is wise who knows his or her rights — both civil and canonical, asks the wise questions, and is familiar with the procedures being followed.

Conclusion

In the ideal world all individuals will be honest, upstanding, virtuous and forthright; those in authority will be wise, sensitive, sincere and courageous. Unfortunately, ours is not an ideal world. It is marred by the shortcomings of our human nature. In the ideal world concern for privacy and confidentiality will not be needed, since wrongdoing on anyone's part will not exist. Until the dawning of that ideal world we mortals are left with the task of negotiating some difficult terrain. This issue of confidentiality is one of those difficult spots. For most religious, the concern is not a great one; their experiences have not taken them onto this territory. But for the minority of religious, a minority that seems these days to be increasing in numbers, the concern for what is being known or said about them is a real one. The best defense for those individuals is, in addition to their upstanding lives and commitment to service, knowledge of their rights and protections under the law, and courage in their vindication.

Elissa Rinere, C.P.

This article originally appeared in *Bulletin on Issues of Religious Law*, Vol. 11, 1995.

IV.
Novitiate

24.
PURPOSE AND PLACE OF THE NOVITIATE: CANONS 646-647

INTRODUCTION

Canon 647 on the novitiate and formation of novices contains the provisions for the place of a valid novitiate. Careful attention should be given to this norm so as not to invalidate the novitiate of the candidate and subsequent religious profession. The conditions for the validity of place concern the purpose and place of the novitiate. I will attempt here to describe current forms of experimentation regarding the novitiate vis-a-vis canon 647 on the place of the novitiate. Hopefully, this discussion will be of some small assistance to major superiors and formation personnel in providing for this significant period of initiation into a religious institute.

I. PURPOSE OF NOVITIATE

The purpose of the novitiate or the beginning of life in a religious institute is to test one's personal vocation with the communal vocation of a particular institute and to incorporate oneself gradually into the life and mission of the religious community. Pope Pius XI observed that to make a novitiate poorly was to build one's religious life on sand. The candidate experiences the particular religious life through the witness of the formation personnel and studies the proper law, history, spirit and wholesome traditions of the institute. Both the formation personnel and the novice test to see if the institute and if the candidate can resolve to live life according to the spirit of the founder or foundress as articulated in the proper law of the institute. For these reasons, the novitiate has always held a place of extreme importance at the beginning of religious life (*Renovationis causam* 4).

Canon 652 provides the content for a course of studies and practices of asceticism which would enable the novice to understand and integrate the values of religious life. Other studies or duties which would not contribute to the formation of the candidate or would be a distraction or a detriment to the serious work of formation are to be discouraged. A qualified director of novices and assistants, if necessary, are to be freed from other assignments both within and beyond the institute to carry out this responsibility in a stable manner (c. 651). The novices should cooperate with these persons in order to prepare for the eventual total gift of themselves to Christ in a perpetual commitment (c. 652, §3). Other members of the religious institute assist through their prayer and witness (c. 652, §4).

II. Place of the Novitiate

Canon 647 provides for the place of the novitiate. The novitiate house is to be erected through a written decree of the supreme moderator of the institute with the consent of the council. For validity, the novitiate must take place in a canonically erected house properly designated for this purpose. While the first section of canon 647, §2 does not state house "of the institute," it should be interpreted as such both from former legislation and from what follows in the canon. Only in particular cases, and by way of exception, by the concession of the supreme moderator with the consent of the council can a novice make a novitiate in another house of the institute under the guidance of an approved religious who assumes the role of the director of novices. A major superior can permit a group of novices to live for a stated period of time in another house of the institute designated by the same superior.

The novitiate house should be chosen wisely with the purpose uppermost in the mind of the superior general and council. It should afford the space, leisure and atmosphere in which the novices can integrate the nature and spirit of the institute while observing the lived example of the director of formation and assistants. The novitiate should be truly reflective of a religious community where the novice can experience and identify with the particular religious lifestyle of the institute. Such experience and study enable the director of novices and candidate to determine his or her suitability for religious life.

III. Recent Forms of Experimentation with the Novitiate

In the early postconciliar period, major superiors saw the need to prepare formation personnel for their most important task. Centers of study for formation directors began to develop in order to assist them in their demanding work. These centers were advantageous not only from academic and formative aspects, but the directors shared insights, prayed together and gradually brought their candidates together from the various institutes for Eucharist, communal penances, classes in spiritual reading and discussions. Major superiors of small religious institutes asked that their novices be permitted to attend the classes given in larger religious congregations which had the advantages of trained professors among their members or the financial resources to procure the same. Novices from smaller institutes would travel to nearby novitiates for courses in liturgy, ecclesiology, spiritual theology and other studies in the consecrated life. Such sharing of classes proved helpful for candidates of both congregations, since it afforded the novices the opportunity to appreciate the unique charism of their own religious institute vis-a-vis the gifts given by the Spirit to the Church through other religious institutes.

With the scarcity of religious vocations and the departures from religious life, institutes have become increasingly unable to provide teachers, facilities and support for their candidates in the formative years. Likewise, institutes of an international character cannot unite their novitiates; for sociocultural conditions and different languages preclude such a common novitiate for their candidates. Their candidates in the United States have more in common with candidates from institutes of the same sociocultural constructs.

Centers of study have been established in close proximity to several novitiates of both men and women religious institutes where major superiors and formation personnel bring their candidates together to share professors, classes and facilities. Novices travel and attend classes with others aspiring to the same essential values of religious life. Classes in Sacred Scripture, liturgy, theology of the vows, the sacraments, ecclesiology and the behavioral sciences all contain theory important to the candidates, intensifying their Christian commitment through a positive response to religious life. These classes do not preclude the studies on the nature, spirit, history and traditions of the particular institute to be taught by qualified persons of the religious institute in the canonically erected novitiate house of each of these religious institutes (*Perfectae caritatis* 21).

Recently, other experiments have developed which could best be described as inter-congregational novitiates. Novices of different religious institutes accompanied by the director of novices live together in a common formation house for the canonical year. Often these religious institutes share the same charism and spirituality. In other instances, one or more novices of one institute live and make the novitiate with the candidates of another institute. It would seem that these two experimentations are not envisioned nor provided for in the present law and would require an indult or permission from the Congregation for Institutes of Consecrated Life and Societies of Apostolic Life.

Some major superiors permit their novices to take advantage of such inter-congregational experiences during the second year of novitiate after the canonical year has been completed. Such an experience would contribute to the novices' broader vision of religious life. It would seem that more study and evaluation of the inter-congregational novitiates of institutes sharing the same charism and spirituality needs to be done. However, the present law with its wise tradition of the place of the novitiate has certain advantages for the formation of the candidate within the boundaries of the institute, without dissipating the energies of the candidates as they are formed in the peculiar lifestyle.

V. Conclusion

Perfectae caritatis 18 states that the renewal of institutes depends for the most part on the formation of their members. It is no easy task today, given the loss of gifted members and the small number of candidates seeking religious life, to provide the solid spiritual and doctrinal preparation for the novice to live a quality religious life. Such a task demands the initiative, resourcefulness and generosity of major superiors, formation personnel and gifted teachers. Many of these are to be commended for their valuable contributions to the formative studies of candidates in various religious institutes. Of singular importance, however, is the lived witness and particular studies in the novitiate community of the institute, as the candidate begins to understand and identify with the nature and spirit of a specific religious institute. This process ultimately leads to an irrevocable union of the candidate's personal call with the communal vocation of the religious community. Major superiors and formation personnel should seek to understand these basic principles of identity and unity in the formative process and do all within their power to effect them in the lives of their potential members.

Rose McDermott, S.S.J.

This article originally appeared in *Bulletin on Issues of Religious Law*, Vol. 5, 1989.

25.
THE INTER-COMMUNITY NOVITIATE

INTRODUCTION

The subject of "inter-community novitiate" is one that has sparked interest because fewer people are entering religious life, and communities have been motivated to look for ways to assure competent formation in a proper atmosphere without devoting too many members to formation and risking the inefficient use of personnel. They believe they can provide a better program by sharing resources than by trying to do it alone. A number of institutes have established an inter-community novitiate for their provinces, but the available information indicates there are only two inter-institute novitiates in the United Sates (novitiates established by several autonomous institutes). These novitiates have been established by institutes with the same charism or tradition. To date, it appears no group of institutes with different charisms have attempted to establish an inter-community novitiate (for example, Benedictines with Dominicans, Franciscans, Marists, etc.) in the USA.

On February 2, 1990, the Congregation for Institutes of Consecrated Life and Societies of Apostolic Life published "Directives on Formation in Religious Institutes." The directives make two statements which relate directly to the subject.

> 100. Inter-institutional collaboration for the formation of young professed, for ongoing formation and for the formation of formators can be effected within the framework of a center. The formation of novices, on the other hand, can only be given under the form of periodic services, since the novitiate community properly so-called must be a homogeneous community proper to each institute. Our dicastery intends to publish a special normative document later on dealing with the establishment of inter-institutional collaboration in the area of formation.

The emphasis here is clearly on a novitiate that is a "homogeneous community proper to each institute." Second:

> 50. [M]aking the novitiate in an inserted community is completely discouraged ... [T]he demands of formation must take precedence over certain apostolic advantages in a poor milieu.

The emphasis here is clearly on a community dedicated to and capable of providing formation.

These two statements may be at cross purposes in some situations where institutes definitely cannot reasonably provide a novitiate community dedicated to formation within the institute.

This study is not an attempt to examine the wisdom or necessity of an inter-community novitiate, but rather to examine the canonical requirements for a novitiate, and especially to determine whether the canons prohibit such an approach. If there is no obstacle in the requirements of a canon, then the question becomes how does an institute proceed in accord with the canon. This process is necessary because, although the canons do not specifically prohibit the establishment of an inter-community novitiate, they are not written in a way that contemplates an inter-community novitiate among autonomous institutes.

Canonical Norms

> 1. Canon 641 — The right of admitting candidates to the novitiate pertains to major superiors according to the norm of proper law.

The right of admission belongs to the major superior. Since admission belongs to the major superior of several different institutes, it raises the question of whether admission standards should be the same or similar for each institute so that novices come from a pre-novitiate background that enables them to begin a common program. Pre-novitiate programs differ widely. Some institutes prefer a longer, more intense program in an attempt to decrease the potential number of departures from novitiate. Others believe that less preparation is necessary and prefer that the weight of initial discernment occur in the novitiate. If the novitiate programs are too disparate, a novice director (or team) may find the class of novices so diverse that common formation is a near-impossible task.

An inter-community novitiate may necessitate a deeper level of communication between the admitting major superiors and the novice director. This may take the form of agreed upon norms by all the institutes in regard to the specific requirements to enter the novitiate. It may even require more dialogue than usual between the major superiors and the novice director so that the director is confident that the people being admitted are properly prepared for novitiate. There may need to be more input than usual from the novice director on whether a candidate is ready for novitiate. The norms should be in place and dialogue assured so that the novice directors are not put into the position of constantly questioning the judgment of the major superior (or vice versa).

Since canon 641 calls for the admission norms to be in proper law, it seems that the basic norms should be fundamental to all the institutes. Individual institutes may have additional norms but common norms protect the viability of the inter-community novitiate.

> 2. Canon 642 - Superiors are to be vigilant about admitting only those who, besides the required age, have health, suitable character and sufficient qualities of maturity to embrace the particular life of the institute; this health, character, and maturity are to be attested to, if necessary by using experts, with due regard for the prescription of canon 220.

The age range, health, character and maturity are specific areas that would usually be the subject of common norms. There is likely to be more diversity over what constitutes the qualities in these areas that pertain to the specific life of the institute, even in cases of a common charism or tradition. These particular qualities need to be formulated and explained so that the novice director understands that this person exhibits the qualities that a particular institute is looking for.

> 3. Canon 643 — §1. One is invalidly admitted to the novitiate:
>
> 1° who has not yet completed the seventeenth year of age;
>
> 2° who is a spouse, during a marriage;
>
> 3° who is presently held by a sacred bond with any institute of consecrated life or who is incorporated in any society of apostolic life, with due regard for the prescription of canon 684;
>
> 4° who enters the institute as a result of force, grave fear or fraud, or whom the superior receives induced in the same way;
>
> 5° who has concealed his or her incorporation in any institute of consecrated life or society of apostolic life.
>
> §2. Proper law can establish other impediments to admission, even for validity, or can add other conditions.

The assurance that none of the canonical impediments exist is the responsibility of the admitting institute. Section 2, however, provides for proper law to establish other impediments or conditions. The institutes may agree to adopt certain impediments or conditions to assure the quality of those admitted. Some of these conditions are probably already present in the admission policies of the institutes. Where there are more similar policies, there is already the basis for additional common impediments or conditions.

The admission standards of canon 644 and canon 645 are to be verified by the admitting institute.

> 4. Canon 646 — The novitiate, by which life in the institute begins, is ordered to this, that the novices better recognize their divine vocation and one which is, moreover, proper to the institute, that they experience the institute's manner of living, that they be formed in mind and heart by its spirit, and that their intention and suitability be tested.

This canon refers to the institute in two important matters. First, a person's vocation is "proper to the institute," and they are to experience "the institute's manner of living." Practically, this means that institutes which have a common charism have a much easier task of forming a person in the vocation of the institute and providing an experience of the institute's manner of living. This would be a much more formidable task for institutes of different traditions, especially in regard to providing an experience of the institute's manner of living.

However, it is not an impossible task for institutes of different traditions. Canon 646 does not limit the experience to the "canonical year." So the institute's manner of living could be specifically experienced during another part of the novitiate program. In addition, periods of time either at the site of an inter-community novitiate or within the institute itself can be arranged during the canonical year so long as they do not violate the norms for the canonical year.

5. Canon 647 — §1. The erection, transfer and suppression of a novitiate house are to take place through a written decree of the supreme moderator of the institute with the consent of his or her council.

§2. In order to be valid, a novitiate must be made in a house properly designated for this purpose. In particular cases and as the exception, by concession of the supreme moderator with the consent of the council, a candidate can make the novitiate in another house of the institute under the guidance of an approved religious who assumes the role of director of novices.

§3. A major superior can permit a group of novices to live for a stated period of time in another house of the institute, designated by the same superior.

§1. This section calls for the supreme moderator to erect the novitiate house. There are two options here for inter-community novitiates. First, one supreme moderator can erect a house, and the major superiors of other institutes could request dispensation for their novices to make the novitiate there. Second, each supreme moderator could erect the same house as the novitiate for their respective institute. There is a question here of whether the house needs to be a house of each institute erected in accord with canon 608 and canon 609. Although §1 does not specifically say the erection of a novitiate house is restricted to a house of the institute, §2, when describing the option of making the novitiate in another house, does describe the other house as "another house of the institute." If the canon is property interpreted as meaning another house of the institute, it means that each major superior would first establish the house as a house of the institute and then each supreme moderator would erect the house as a novitiate house.

There may be a question whether the same house can be a house of several institutes. The language of the canon does not prohibit it; however, it is recognized that the rights that accompany the erection of a religious house (c. 611) speak of those rights in terms of "the institute." The more flexible interpretation may be somewhat dependent on the question of the wisdom of establishing an inter-community novitiate.

§2. The option of providing another house as a novitiate would be helpful even in the case of an inter-community novitiate if there were reasons not to use the inter-community novitiate for a novice.

§3. In the case of providing a common experience for the inter-community novices, two steps would be required. First, the house is to be "another house of the institute." This would require the ability of each institute to name one house as its house (see comment on c. 647, §1) or a dispensation to send the novices to a house which is not a house of the institute. If the question of the house can be successfully dealt with, then each major superior needs to give permission and designate the period of time.

> 6. Canon 650 — §1. The scope of the novitiate demands that the novices be formed under the guidance of a director according to the program of training to be defined by the proper law.
>
>> §2. The governance of novices is reserved to one director under the authority of the major superiors.

§1. The novitiate program is to be defined by proper law. Since several institutes are coming together, the program of training needs to be a common program and, therefore, the proper law describing the program should be adopted by each institute. Although each institute probably has unique interests, it is doubtful if a variety of unique interests could be adequately addressed during the short duration of a novitiate. These interests will of necessity probably be left to the institute itself.

§2. The governance is left to one director under the authority of the major superiors. In an inter-community novitiate, this means that the director is under the authority of each major superior. It could be fragmenting to have diverse expectations from each major superior. This is an area in which major superiors need to arrive at their expectations for the director.

> 7. Canon 651 — §1. The director of novices is to be a member of the institute who has professed perpetual vows and is legitimately designated.
>
>> §2. If there is a need, assistants can be given to the director to whom they are subject regarding the governance of the novitiate and the program of training.
>
>> §3. Members who have been carefully prepared and who, not impeded by other duties, can carry out this duty fruitfully and in a stable manner are to be in charge of the training of novices.

§1. There are two important concerns in the appointment of a director. First, the director must be a member of the institute. Second, it is not possible for the person chosen as director to be a member of each institute. There are two options here. The first was mentioned previously: that one superior name the director and establish the novitiate, and all other superiors obtain dispensations for their novices to attend that novitiate. The second would be for each superior to name that person as the director and obtain a dispensation for naming a non-member of the institute.

§2. All novitiates, including an inter-community novitiate, are to have one director, and the director may have assistants. The code does not provide for co-directors, or directors with equal authority, even if several institutes contribute personnel for the novitiate. Directors with equal authority would require a dispensation.

8. Canon 653 — §1. A novice can freely leave an institute; moreover the competent authority of the institute can dismiss a novice.

§2. When the novitiate is completed, a novice, if judged suitable, is to be admitted to temporary profession; otherwise the novice is to be dismissed. If there is a doubt about the novice's suitability, the time of probation can be extended by the major superior according to the norm of proper law, but not more than six months.

§1. The question of dismissing a novice is a sensitive issue. Institutes have different practices. Some leave the decision in the hands of the directors (the canon refers to competent authority) while others leave it to the major superior based on the principle that the authority who admits should be the authority who dismisses. Institutes establishing an inter-community novitiate need clear norms in this area. If authority is reserved to each major superior and the director recommends dismissal and the major superior disagrees, it may result in a very negative atmosphere, since the director may be forced to deal with a novice the director believes should not be there.

If authority to dismiss resides in the director, the major superior may believe that the institute is losing potential members because of bad decisions. Regardless of how much communication is structured into the system, there must be some agreement on who has the authority to dismiss.

§2. Extending time in the novitiate belongs to the major superior. Although the authority is designated, the area is similar to dismissal if the director and major superior are in disagreement. Of course, if the canonical year is complete, the time and place of extension can be left to the major superior and need not take place at the inter-community novitiate.

As noted above, the canons do not contemplate inter-institute novitiates and — depending on the structure chosen by the institute — certain dispensations may be needed. One way to avoid either annual or periodic requests for dispensations would be to develop a program with all the decisions assigned to various superiors and then request approval of the plan from CICLSAL with all the necessary dispensations.

Inter-community novitiates are likely to become attractive solutions to resolve the problems of providing the best possible formation in spite of limited resources and few novices. It is clear that even with a flexible interpretation of the canons, some dispensation(s) will be needed depending on the choice(s) of the institutes desiring to form an inter-community novitiate. The whole question awaits the publication of the norms on inter-institutional collaboration in formation. Meanwhile, the sparse but important activity in this area shows the necessity of developing norms that allow institutes to respond to the responsibility of providing appropriate formation.

Jordan Hite, T.O.R.

This article originally appeared in *Bulletin on Issues of Religious Law*, Vol. 7, 1991.

26.
ADMISSION TO THE NOVITIATE:
CANON 643, §1, 2° – IMPEDIMENT OF
EXISTING MARRIAGE BOND

During recent years, major superiors, vocation directors and formation personnel have experienced the phenomenon of persons who are or have been married applying for entrance to religious life. Frequently those interviewing such candidates must deal with significant pastoral and canonical issues.

I. CESSATION OF MARRIAGE BOND

There is no canonical impediment for persons whose marriage bond has ceased to exist because: a) the spouse has died or b) the marriage has been annulled or dissolved by the Church. In such cases there is no marriage; hence, the applicant is free to apply for admission to the novitiate.

While this person is free from the canonical impediment of an existing marriage bond, he or she must pass the same scrutiny as any other candidate. It is well for those interviewing the person to keep in mind that this candidate has lived an intimate *communio vitae*. How the person lived this close interpersonal relationship will certainly shed light on his or her potential to live community in religious life. In the case of one whose marriage has been annulled, a copy of the decree should be requested. The reasons for the annulment should be a significant consideration in the decision to admit the person to the novitiate.

II. EXISTING MARRIAGE BOND

Regarding those who are married, canon 643, §1, 2° of the 1983 Code repeats canon 542, §1 of the 1917 Code:

> Canon 643, §1: One is invalidly admitted to the novitiate:
> 2° who is a spouse, during a marriage:

The law addresses the person in a valid marriage whose spouse is still living, and whose marriage has not been annulled or dissolved by the Church. The bond of marriage clearly constitutes a diriment impediment to admission to religious life and would invalidate the novitiate and subsequent religious profession. A civil divorce, permanent separation, and/or the permission of the spouse to enter religious life do not free the person for admission to the novitiate of a religious institute.

If it is reasonably certain that the person is otherwise suitable for the religious institute, the impediment should be dealt with before the person is admitted into a candidacy or pre-novitiate program. The candidate should be advised to make an appointment with a person in the marriage tribunal to determine the possibility of an annulment of the marriage or the reasonable assurance that the dispensation from the impediment may be granted. If the procedure for an annulment is recommended, the formation personnel should encourage the person to pursue this possibility.

If there is no hope of an annulment, and the marital union seems irretrievably broken due to infidelity of the spouse or for some other grave reason, the candidate can petition the Apostolic See for a dispensation from the impediment of the existing marriage bond in order to enter religious life. Before this request is granted, the person must have a decree of permanent separation granted by the diocesan bishop. This would preclude the former partner from attempting to reclaim conjugal privileges once the person pursues his or her vocation in religious life.

The following should be included in the documentation sent to Rome:

1. A petition from the candidate seeking admission to the novitiate of the particular religious institute requesting the dispensation from the impediment of the existing marriage bond. The petition should include a brief history of the marriage, the cause of the breakdown, the number of children, their ages and provisions for life. The petitioner should give an honest assessment of his or her contribution to the marital failure.

2. A statement from the superior general of the religious institute indicating his/her willingness to receive the petitioner if the dispensation is granted.

3. A copy of the decree of divorce, since this document often settles financial and other civil matters involved.

4. A copy of the decree of permanent separation granted by the diocesan bishop.

5. Copies of the marriage and baptismal certificates of the petitioner, spouse and children.

6. If possible, the marriage certificate of the spouse if he or she has remarried or a written statement from the spouse stating that he or she has no intent to resume marital rights.

The petitioner should have some canonical assistance in preparing the brief for the Apostolic See. Much frustration can be avoided for the person and the religious institute if competent assistance is sought in ample time.

This is a relatively new experience in the area of admission to religious life. However, skillful interviewing, proper criteria and canonical counsel will assist those making decisions to admit such persons to religious life. Needless to say, abandonment of serious commitments and responsibilities, or the inability to relate with another human being, should send up warning signals to vocation and formation personnel and major superiors. In efforts to assist candidates in dealing with canon 643, §1, 2° — the diriment impediment of an existing marriage bond, canon 642 must not be forgotten. This canon requires the vigilance of superiors in admitting only those candidates who have the suitable character and sufficient qualities of maturity requisite for the particular life of the religious institute.

Rose McDermott, S.S.J.

This article originally appeared in *Bulletin on Issues of Religious Law*, Vol. 7, 1991.

Authors

CLAUDIA BARBRE, R.S.M., J.C.L., is Defender of the Bond and Advocate in the Tribunal of the Diocese of Portland, Maine.

MELANIE BAIR, O.S.F., J.C.D., teaches at The Catholic University of Korea, Seoul, Korea.

RICHARD A. HILL, S.J., J.C.D., is Professor Emeritus of Canon Law, Jesuit School of Theology, Berkeley, California.

JORDAN HITE, T.O.R., J.D., J.C.L., ministers at St. John the Baptist Church in Wagner, South Dakota.

SHARON HOLLAND, I.H.M., J.C.D., is an official with the Congregation for Institutes of Consecrated Life and for Societies of Apostolic Life, Rome.

DAVID M. HYNOUS, O.P, J.C.D., is Procurator General for the Order of Preachers, Rome.

ROSE MCDERMOTT, S.S.J., is Assistant Professor of Canon Law, The Catholic University of America, Washington, District of Columbia.

ELIZABETH MCDONOUGH, O.P., J.C.D., is a canonical consultant, based in Henderson, North Carolina.

MARGARET MARY MODDE, O.S.F., J.C.D., is an associate with the firm of McDermott, Will & Emery, Chicago, Illinois.

FRANCIS G. MORRISEY, O.M.I., J.C.D., is Professsor of Canon Law, Saint Paul University, Ottawa.

ELLEN O'HARA, C.S.J., J.C.D., J.D., is a consultant in canon law and practices civil law in Salt Lake City, Utah.

JAMES H. PROVOST is Professor of Canon Law, The Catholic University of America, Washington, District of Columbia.

ELISSA RINERE, C.P., J.C.D., is a Judge for the Metropolitan Tribunal of the Archdiocese of Los Angeles.

FRED SACKETT, O.M.I., J.C.D., is a Judge for the Appellate Court, San Antonio, Texas.

ROSEMARY SMITH, S.C., J.C.D., is Director of Women's Advocacy for the Congregation of the Sisters of Charity of the Incarnate Word, Houston, Texas.

MADELINE WELCH, O.S.U., J.D., J.C.L., serves in congregational leadership for the Ursuline Provincialate, Eastern Province of the United States.

INDEX

Active/passive voice
  during exclaustration 61
  during transfer to new institute 67

Admission
  character 129
  health of candidate 128-129
  maturity 129
  pre-existing marriage
    bond 160-162

Annulment
  admission to novitiate 161

Apostolate
  agreement between institute and
    diocesan bishop 139-140
  associate members 81
  contracts 39-40
  corporate 39-40
  diocesan bishop 38-41, 74-76
  in name of institute 36
  individual apostolates 40
  removal of religious from office 40

Archives 141, 143

Assignment to diocese 135, 138-139

Associate membership 77-84
  apostolate 81
  canonical considerations 80
  evaluation 83
  financial considerations 83
  participation in governance 79

Authority 12

Autonomy of institute 138, 139

Brother superior in clerical
  institute 30-31

Calumny 125

Canon Law Society of America 49

Canonical advisor 48-49

Catholic schools
  belonging to religious 39
  diocesan policies 39
  visitation by diocesan bishop 39

Charism 51, 57, 98
  transfer to new institute 58

Charitable subsidy 62, 63, 85-91

Chastity 7

Clerical institute
  brother as superior 30-31
  definition 70

Clerical pontifical institutes 29

Cloistered nuns
  permission to leave cloister 37

Collaboration in government 11

Collegial Governance
  (*see* Governance)

Common good of the institute 143

Common life 34, 36, 57

Confidentiality 14, 124-134
  right to confidentiality 142-147
  right to one's reputation
    124-126, 136
  right to privacy 126-128
  secrecy 125

164

sharing information with
   diocesan officials 76
spiritual director 131

Congregation for Institutes of Consecrated Life and for Societies of Apostolic Life
   imposed/involuntary exclaustration 60-61
   questions frequently asked of 4-8
   review of proper law 4-6

Consecrated virgins (*see* Order of Virgins)

Constitutions 6
   necessary norms 6

Contemplative/monastic institutes
   definition 70

Contracts for apostolate 39-40, 75

Councils
   required 11
   advice 13
   consent 13

Counseling 57 (*see* Therapy)

Delegation 29
   dispensing powers 30

Departure
   charitable subsidy 62, 63, 85-91
   pensions 88

Difficult religious 57-64
   intervention 57
   (*see* Counseling, Therapy)

Diocesan bishop 69-76
   apostolate, oversight of 38

Diocesan institute
   definition 70
   diocesan bishop 74

Dismissal; 62-63
   automatic 46
   confirmation of 46
   decree of 45
   mandatory 46
   process 46
   temporary health benefits 63

Dispensation from vows 42-47

Domination power 28

Dominican *donati* 77

Dress 7
   (*see* Habit)

Ecclesiastical office 28

Elections 8, 15-16, 17-25
   active/passive voice 16
   diocesan bishop 17
   direct 15-16
   discernment 21
   elector, rights of 21
   information exchange 20
   mail ballots 16
   non-acceptance 24-25
   postulation 22-24
   preparation 20
   proxy 16
   secrecy 19
   transfer to new institute 67
   universal suffrage 21-22

Equity (*see* Charitable subsidy)

Eremitic/anchoritic life 93
   admission/formation 96-97
   finances 97-98

Essential Elements 10, 11

Eucharist 7, 8

Exclaustration 34, 42, 58-59
  cloistered nuns 35
  duration of necessity 60-61
  effects of 61
  financial assistance 62
  habit 7, 34, 45, 61
  imposed 8, 44-45, 59
  notification of local ordinary 61
  voluntary 59, 67

Files
  personal 127, 130-131
  personnel 145-146

Formation 7, 64

Governance
  laity 26-32
  power of 10, 29
  collegial 11, 12-14

Habit 7
  during exclaustration 34, 45, 61

Hermits 93, 96-98

House (*domus religiosa*) 74

Impediment of existing marriage bond
  admission to novitiate 160-162
  annulment decree 160
  dispensation from impediment
    by Apostolic See 161-162

Incomplete term 24

Income 86

Individual Apostolates
and written agreement 40

Indult of departure 42-43

Institute's relationship with diocese
and confidentiality 135-141

Intercommunity novitiate 152, 154-159

Internal Forum 126

Laity
  governance 26-32
  lay judges 27
  lay superior 26

Lay institute
  definitions 70

Leave of absence 34-35, 58
  active/passive voice 37
  indefinite 36-37

Letters of recommendation 126-127, 146-157
  internal forum 126

Major superior
  confirmation of election 16
  elections 17-125
  incomplete term 24
  title 17
  underlying values 18-20

Medical history 127
  medical records 145
  mental health records 144

Membership 46
  disruptive member 46
  marginal 46

Merger 24, 50-56
  decree 55
  definition 51
  diocesan bishop 54
  options for members 53, 55
  process 52-56
  reasons 50

Monastic institute 21

INDEX

Mutual Relations
  (*Mutuae relationes*) 12

New forms of consecrated
life 83-84, 95, 98
  as private association 99

New religious institutes 94

Nominal religious 64

Non-canonical groups 95

Novitiate 7
  admission 155-156, 160-162
  departure 159
  director 158
  dismissal 159
  forms of experimentation 151-152
  inter-community/congregational
    152, 154-159
  length 159
  purpose 150, 156-157
  place 151, 157-158

Obedience, vow of 12

Order of virgins (Consecrated Virgins)
93-98

Particular law (Proper law) 4, 69
  Direct election of superiors 15-16

Pedophilia 133, 139-140

Penance (Reconciliation) 8

Pension
  departed members 88

Perpetual Profession 5

Personnel files
  grave behavioral problems 65

Pontifical institute 70
  diocesan bishop 74

Postulation 22-24

Potestas regiminis 26-32

Potestas jurisdictionis (see *Potestas regiminis*)

Poverty, vow of 7

Power of governance/jurisdiction (see
Potestas regiminis)

Power of orders 26-32

Previous marriage bond (*see* Impediment
of existing marriage bond)

Privacy, right to 126-128, 136-137, 142

Private apostolates 41

Private association 99

Proper law (*see* Particular law)

Psychological testing of candidates 127,
128-129, 131

Public office 113-121
  1917 Code provisions 114-115
  1983 Code provisions 115-119

Recent developments in consecrated life
92-100

Reputation
  right to 124-126, 136
  slander 125
  calumny 125

Secrecy 125

Secular institutes, new foundation 94

167

Selection of canon lawyer 48-49
   fees 49
   interpretation of canon law 48

Separation from institute 8, 42-47
   (*see* Dismissal
        Dispensation
        Dismissal
        Exclaustration
        Indult of departure)

Sexual misconduct 137, 139
   statement from major superior to diocese 139-140

Society of apostolic life
   new foundation 94

Spirituality 12 (*see* Charism)

Sponsorship 101-112
   Catholic identity 105-108
   governance issues 107
   liability 108-110
   role of the laity 110-111
   tutelle 111-112

Superior 28
   duties 10-11
   intermediary superior 8
   obligation of confidentiality 137
   office 10
   personal authority 10-11, 12
   privacy of individual 11
   title 17

Supreme moderator, direct election 15-16

Team ministry as form of governance
   not an option 14

Temporary vows, expiration 43

Therapy (*see* Counseling)
   previous treatment 132
   rights of superiors 132-133
   requesting a member to enter into 133, 138-139
   refusal by member 133, 138-139

Third orders 77-78
   see Associate membership

Transfer to new institute 42, 43-44, 66-68, 131-132
   reason 66-67
   permission 67
   probationary period 67-68
   financial considerations 68
   return to institute 68

Troublesome religious
   (*see* Difficult religious)

Union 24, 50-56
   decree 55
   definition 51
   diocesan bishop 54
   options for members 53, 55
   process 52-53
   reasons for 50-52

Universal suffrage 21-22

Vacancy of office 24

Visitation by diocesan bishop 69

Vocational crisis 34-35
   (*see* Leave of absence)

Vows, formula 6